Red Dirt Women

Red Dirt Women

AT HOME ON THE OKLAHOMA PLAINS

Susan Kates

Foreword by Rilla Askew

∾

To JD—my first lover —
who taught me to love big
even if it hurts a lot later...
Thank you for walking into
the Hilton hotel at just the
right moment. Without you, so much
might have turned out different.
Thank you for the path—and
some of the best memories
of a lifetime. Susan ♡

UNIVERSITY OF OKLAHOMA PRESS : NORMAN

This book is published with the generous assistance of the Wallace C. Thompson Endowment Fund, University of Oklahoma Foundation.

Unless otherwise noted, all photographs in this book are by Susan Kates.

Epigraph quotation is from *The House on Mango Street*. Copyright © 1984 by Sandra Cisneros. Published by Vintage Books, a division of Random House, Inc., and in hardcover by Alfred A. Knopf in 1994. By permission of Susan Bergholz Literary Services, New York, N.Y., and Lamy, N.Mex. All rights reserved.

Library of Congress Cataloging-in-Publication Data

Kates, Susan, 1961–
  Red dirt women : at home on the Oklahoma plains / Susan Kates ; foreword by Rilla Askew.
    p. cm.
  Includes bibliographical references.
  ISBN 978-0-8061-4359-0 (pbk. : alk. paper) 1. Kates, Susan, 1961–
2. Women authors, American—Homes and haunts. 3. Group identity—Oklahoma. 4. Oklahoma—Social conditions. 5. Oklahoma—Social life and customs. 6. Women—Oklahoma—Biography. I. Title. II. Title: Home on the Oklahoma plains.
  PS3611.A7884R43 2013
  814'.6—dc23

                                              2012039756

The paper in this book meets the guidelines for permanence and durability of the Committee on Production Guidelines for Book Longevity of the Council on Library Resources, Inc. ∞

1 2 3 4 5 6 7 8 9 10

For Carson

You can never have too much sky.
You can fall asleep
and wake up drunk on sky,
and sky can keep you safe
when you are sad.
  —Sandra Cisneros, *The House on Mango Street*

Contents

Foreword, by Rilla Askew   xi

Introduction: Prairie Women, Prairie Places   3

Adoption Story   9

Great Plains Salvage   27

Miss Dorrie at Big Sky   37

Girls in the Ring   47

The Bird Watcher   59

Casinoland   69

Queens of the Pioneer Outback   81

Roller Dolls   93

Lady of Jade   103

The Ideal Home   115

References   129

Acknowledgments   133

Foreword

Rilla Askew

When I first met Susan Kates in 2004, I recognized in her a fellow writer in love with the plains. We were introduced by our mutual friend Catherine Hobbs, a native Oklahoman and avid bird watcher, who is marvelously profiled in one of the essays here. Susan's enthusiasm for my home territory and its inhabitants was immediately apparent: infectious, kinetic, authentic, deeply felt. I knew her to be an eastern transplant, but I couldn't have imagined then that her passion for "the great spaces and windy light" of the southern plains was in fact a learned love. She seemed to me such a natural adoptee of Oklahoma that it wasn't until I read her writings that I came to understand how distinctly her knowledge of and enthusiasm for the character and characters of red dirt country are the consequence of a complex and riveting personal journey. As these pages make clear, that passage hasn't been without its missteps and adventures, but the resulting narrative is the compelling story of an outsider and admitted agoraphobe who has learned to cherish the wide-open spaces, endless sky, and perpetual wind of plains country, and to appreciate with a keen observing eye the unique culture of a place and its citizens—most particularly its women.

I've been writing about plainswomen, pioneer women, red dirt women in my fiction all my writing life, always with a view to oppose stereotype. Those of us who write about this frequently stereotyped part of the country have to work hard to resist overused images and worn tropes—a constant challenge for anyone writing in the shadow of Ma Joad, with her poor grammar and earthy wisdom, and the iconic figure of the Pioneer Woman as represented in Bryant Baker's famous statue: bonneted, beautiful, striding forth holding her young son's hand to heroically meet the dangers and difficulties of life on the plains. In *Red Dirt Women: At Home on the Oklahoma Plains*, Susan Kates turns the traditional image of the pioneer woman on its head. In fresh, surprising ways, she reveals contemporary Oklahoma women to be as complex and sturdy and subtly varied as the landscape and culture they come from; she makes clear that their experiences and worldviews are far from monolithic—and she does this through the deft interweaving of her own story with the lives of these red dirt women.

What makes this volume so unique is the way Kates combines elements of memoir and reportage, the personal essay and the journalistic essay, along with the entertaining insights of the character sketch, to create a rich examination of character and place. She is not shy to express the sense of vulnerability she felt on the open plains when she first immigrated to Oklahoma, the uncertainties and miscues that occur when we bump up against an unfamiliar culture. Kates's breadth of scholarship, her humor and keen eye for detail broaden and illuminate what we think we know about pioneer women. The result is a wonderful evocation of contemporary plainswomen's engagement with the land and its history, an arresting examination of the gravitational pull of the West as a place of immigration and emigration, an endless source for the literary imagination, and, as in Kates's own experience, a quest for home. Susan Kates's personal journey of discovery as she encounters these red dirt women, and the peace she's made with treeless terrain and great skies, make for a wonderfully compelling story. I invite you to enjoy the journey.

Red Dirt Women

Introduction

Prairie Women, Prairie Places

In her chronicle of life in Kenya—one of the great grasslands of the world—Isak Dinesen explains that it is impossible to live any place for a time and remain unaltered by one's surroundings. "It does not even make much difference," she says, "whether you have more good or bad things to say of it, it draws your mind to it, by a mental law of gravitation." In the early part of the twentieth century, the Danish-born writer moved to a farm near Nairobi to run a coffee plantation. There, she was transformed by the wind, a clear view of the sky, and the white gnarled arms of trees reaching sadly upward. In that spare landscape she came to know herself in the ways people do when they are forced to empty themselves of their previous connections and meet themselves on new terms, in new territory.

I did not know that moving to Oklahoma would alter me in the ways Dinesen describes. I had never experienced that geographical voodoo exerted by a new place on a person's central nervous system. Here, in this unfamiliar environment, different light, weather, and landscapes replaced those I had previously known.

Oklahoma possesses a varied topography: there are hills and green belts and wetlands, and the arid western portion of the Panhandle near Black Mesa is almost a desert. In the southern part of Oklahoma they call Little Dixie, there are alligators and swamps. It is altogether another ecosystem. But I came to the prairie and it was the prairie where I found myself dislocated and definitely not "at home."

I feel vulnerable on the open lands. There are few trees, and the sunlight exposes everything like a shameless mother. Despite this stark view, there is comfort in the landscape. Trees are crooked and bent by the wind, but they stand against the gusts. In the late afternoon sun with the grass rising out of red dirt bluffs, there is an orange hue that soothes homesickness.

As pleasing as the warm, lovely western light is, I could not, for some time, call the Oklahoma plains home. The Great Plains simply didn't figure into a long-term domestic equation. I did not imagine that if ever I put down roots it would be in the midst of religious conservatism, a flat grassland vista, and chicken-fried everything. Roots were what dull people had. Roots would strangle you if you didn't shake off the tether. One of my college diaries claims Bessie Smith's "Young Woman's Blues" lyrics as a philosophy for living: "No time to marry, no time to settle down / I'm a young woman and ain't done runnin' around." One who has settled down has ended her days as exile, refugee, sojourner, pilgrim, or vagabond. I made a conscious pledge to roam far from marriage, children, and life in one place.

But as this book makes clear, that did not happen. There must have been a day I realized I could never leave the enormity of sky and intense light on the prairie. Perhaps when my husband and I adopted our son, a native Oklahoman, we became rooted in his birthplace.

I know, however, that I could never have made a home in plains country without the women I've met along the way. Just as the prairie is a landscape all its own, Oklahoma women are unique. They are shaped by the weather, the land, and its history. The Oklahoma women in these essays have taught me about birds and barrel racing, babies, and bingo. Some of them have become my friends and others have guided me in the process of putting down Great Plains roots.

Before I moved to Oklahoma, I knew little about the state, and whatever scanty ideas I had about the region came mostly from Dorothea Lange's Farm Security Administration photographs and John Steinbeck's *The Grapes of Wrath*. Ragged men, women, and children stare out of Lange's pictures, their faces gaunt, aged by poverty and displacement. They are the real-life Joads, who suffer increasingly bad luck and disappointment. Both Lange and Steinbeck tell stories of individuals "dusted out" from their farms and forced to migrate west in a long, unforgettable exodus to California. Such portraits of destitute Americans, victims of the Great Depression and the Dust Bowl, mark a particular period in U.S. history of hunger and hopelessness. Interestingly, neither Lange nor Steinbeck ever lived in Oklahoma, yet their singular vision of the state—documented in photographs and narrative—looms large in the American consciousness to this day.

Certainly one of the dominant themes of Oklahoma history is migration. If you consider the forced relocation of more than 46,000 American Indians, members of the Five Civilized Tribes, to Oklahoma following the shameful Indian Removal Act of 1830; the Land Run of 1889 and the Dust Bowl exodus of the 1930s; as well as the large number of people who moved out of the state after the oil bust of the 1980s, it is not hard to see why migration is part of Oklahoma lore. While such displacements may reflect a portion of the state's history, they do not do it justice. To tell a story about the only state in the union with the sound of *home* in its name, it is necessary to talk about those who have stayed and put down roots, not those who left Oklahoma or merely passed through it on the way to somewhere else. And for me, it is crucial to talk about the women, ordinary women who have exposed me to the treasures of the state, among them rose rocks, fried okra, and the glory of the scissor-tailed flycatcher!

But what does it mean to write about "ordinary" Oklahoma women? As Sandra Schackel observes in *Western Women's Lives*, the image of the Caucasian pioneer mother in a sunbonnet "is deeply symbolic, is part of the powerful, gendered myth of the West embedded in American culture." Schackel argues that many scholars and writers have done little to disrupt this myth. Some individuals may think of Oklahoma women in terms of the rosy Technicolor Laurey Williams played by Shirley Jones in *Oklahoma!* This image, like the pioneer women in sunbonnets or the bedraggled Dust Bowl mothers in photographs, does little to shape an understanding of how diverse Oklahoma plainswomen have always been.

In *Women of Oklahoma, 1890–1920*, Linda Reese works against the image of the Caucasian pioneer mother in a sunbonnet, as she explains how Indian women, black women, and white women settlers "lived the history of the West," shaping the character and values of their husbands and children. Her book enriches western history and helps us see that women influenced the cultures of the West and the Great Plains in very specific ways—through needlework, cooking, child-rearing, and other ethnic and regional practices.

Reese portrays how American Indians marched on the Trail of Tears, how African American "Exodusters" fled the South in the late nineteenth and early twentieth centuries, and how immigrants from Russia and Eastern Europe sought a plot of land to call their own. She celebrates the ethnic diversity and regional complexities of all these women who arrived on the plains of Oklahoma searching for home.

I came to understand Oklahoma plainswomen by reading about Kate Barnard, Angie Debo, Caroline Henderson, Ada Lois Sipuel Fisher, Wilma Mankiller, and other extraordinary women from various backgrounds. These women faced considerable obstacles in a state that didn't think much of women who tried to enter politics or academe, or stake a claim on a Panhandle homestead alone. Oklahoma is where Barnard advocated for American Indian children, where Debo told the story of what whites did to the Indians, where Henderson remained steadfast on her homestead through drought, grasshoppers, the Dust Bowl, and the Depression, where Sipuel Fisher became the first African American woman to enter law school at the University of Oklahoma, and where Mankiller became the first female chief of the Cherokee Nation.

While the names of these and other women are increasingly prevalent in Oklahoma history, the female voices in these essays are much more ordinary. Even so, they have a collective spirit that unites them to all the great women of the past who emerged on the Great Plains to confront a series of adversarial conditions. The women in this book are cowgirls, Vietnamese immigrants, Panhandle Pioneer Days Queens, rollergirls, American Indian casino players, caretakers of children and birds. They have a distinct relationship to Oklahoma and its various cultures. Like me, they are moved, shaped, and ultimately anchored by rhythms of place. I am grateful to have found myself among women who live between the flat land and the sky, among women who have shown me regional treasures so sweet, they fill up my life and grace the immensity of the prairie.

Susan and Violet. Photograph by Crickett Knowlton.

Adoption Story

⟡

The first time I meet Violet's Aunt Crickett, she tells a Bible story to her pregnant niece. It is from First Kings, verses 16–28: Wise Solomon is dispatched to decide a dispute between two bereft mothers who lay claim to the same baby. He solves the dilemma by requesting a sword. "Divide the living child in two," Solomon instructs, "and give half to the one, and half to the other." The *real* mother (a phrase that will haunt me throughout this adoptive journey) is horrified by the pronouncement. She exclaims, "O my lord, give that woman the living child, and in no way slay it: *she* is the mother thereof." The infant is returned to the biological mother because Solomon knows that only the natural mother would give the baby up to let it live.

Crickett finishes in a grave voice. It occurs to me that she offers this narrative in support of Violet's decision to allow my husband and me to adopt her baby. The story seems odd, though, given that Solomon returns the child to the biological mother in the end. But Crickett, who is a devout Pentecostal, tells her niece, "If you are willing, like the woman in the Bible, to give this baby up, someday he will thank you for a good life." The

9

aunt is not confident that her niece can mother this child, given that Violet already has a two-year-old son that she has sometimes neglected. I look at the petite teenager folding laundry for some indication of her response to the aunt's narrative. But Violet looks down and places a towel nonchalantly on a pile of others. Like me, the aunt is pushing forty, but unlike me, she is great with child. Crickett wears a gold cross around her neck—her blond hair flipped back from her face, Farrah Fawcett–style, in 1980s waves. Both aunt and niece have demonstrated considerable fertility over the years. In a matter of weeks they will have given birth to a total of six children between them. They also profess to have had a number of miscarriages. I, on the other hand, have found baby-making quite a challenge.

My quest for a child began years earlier with doctors who, thanks to laparoscopic photography, were able to capture color pictures of my diseased ovaries and those failed messengers, the fallopian tubes. After drugs that made me sick and "reproductive technology" that did not take, my husband Frank and I find ourselves consulting adoption lawyers.

My desperate wish is that someone would put a baby in a basket on my front porch, ring the doorbell, and run away like they do in the movies. I think about Moses, pushed into the reeds by his biological mother, adopted by the Pharaoh's daughter, and raised as her own son to become the leader of the Israelites. I take walks near a pond by my house and imagine how happy I would be if I found a baby in a floating bassinet made of sticks the way the Pharaoh's daughter did. Instead I am childless, one of the duped generation of career women who thought fertility would last forever, or at least until forty (If Madonna could do it, why not I?). Standing in line at Wal-Mart, I am resentful of women whose shopping carts are full of children reaching for candy or squabbling with one another at the checkout.

And then a phone call changes everything.

A good-ole-boy Oklahoma City lawyer telephones with plans to introduce us to a young couple. I dress for the audition of potential parent by trying to look stable, but not dull. Hip, but not trendy. Financially responsible, not snobbishly rich.

On the day of our first meeting at the attorney's office, I see that Violet is a slight girl with long chestnut hair and hazel eyes. She could be any schoolgirl, but she has been in no one's class since seventh grade. Her boyfriend, Dusty, has his right arm in a cast (I will later learn from punching out a window while doing lethal amounts of methamphetamines). His unruly blond hair sticks out beneath a ball cap. Despite the light goatee that could be read as a gesture of rebellious masculinity, he does not look tough. A skull-and-bones tattoo flexes across his bare shoulder with a caption that reads *Lucky*. They tell us they have been together off and on since Violet was fifteen. In a stormy relationship that already has resulted in the birth of one baby, they determine they cannot afford another.

The lawyer holds a crumpled piece of paper with large curly-cued handwriting. "Violet has some questions she would like to ask you," he says, pronouncing "yew" in a drawl that makes him sound like a preacher instead of an attorney. *Have you ever been abused? Have you ever been in jail? Do you drink or use drugs?* I am conscious of a lump in my throat produced by sadness for Violet that she is in a position to need these questions answered. At the same moment I am indignant and sorry for myself that I must be asked such questions in order to become a mother. In this instant I learn that adoption will not be a clean or easy process, but there is no way I can understand yet how truly messy it will be. "I want to get to know you," Violet insists earnestly. "I don't want to just hand *baby* to you at the hospital" (she says patting her stomach). "*I have to know you*," she emphasizes in a voice that sounds brave for a minute before it trails off again.

Getting to know you is the theme of open adoption. Open adoption is a relatively recent, and, by some people's account, radical process in which the birth parents and the adoptive parents form a relationship brokered by lawyers or social workers. As we sign up for this procedure, it feels hazardous, and I understand why many people pursue foreign adoption in Russia, China, or Timbuktu, where the chance of encountering the birth parents is much less likely.

But I am glad that we have come a long way from hiding pregnant women in homes for unwed mothers and whisking infants away abruptly and destructively from birth parents. Oddly enough, a woman who chooses adoption over abortion receives little acknowledgement in a nation where mothers and motherhood are sacred. On a recent TV show about celebrity adoptions, Rosie O'Donnell was the only featured parent to express any appreciation to the ones who had made it all possible. "I am the beneficiary of other women's tremendous generosity," she said. It was the first time I could recall anyone using the adjective *generous* to describe someone who relinquished a child for adoption. *Unwed mother* and *woman in trouble* are terms that more easily come to mind. Voices of birth parents have more often been silenced. These individuals are supposed to disappear gracefully, forget, and go on with their lives. They are often the ghosts that haunt adoptive families: fearsome kidnappers or fantasy parents, sources of hidden genetic defects, holders of the ever-elusive key to history and identity.

Over the months as I get to know Violet, I come to think of her as a rescuer, someone who might, depending on the outcome, rescue me from childlessness, but certainly someone who, on many days, shakes me from my own self-absorption and self-pity. Abandoned by her own mother, raised in the midst of alcoholism, domestic violence, and extreme poverty, Violet is struggling to do the right thing, whatever that may be. She tells me that she does not want any child of hers to endure what she had to as a kid, when she was left to wander the streets of Sulphur eating at the Helping Hands Mission after her mother had disappeared and there was no sight of her or her next meal. Violet compares herself to friends who are living out the legacies of their neglectful parents and pauses thoughtfully: "A few of my friends called me a 'baby seller' the other day. These are people," she proclaims in an injured tone, "who live in filth and do drugs in front of their children."

I have met these friends, two in particular named Carolyn and Cheyenne. They are sitting in the living room of her current apartment smoking cigarettes one afternoon when I come to visit. They despise me, though I have brought along some purses I thought I might pass on to them the way my girlfriends and I trade our wares around when we tire of them. But I should have known better. These girls assume I am trying to buy Violet's baby with designer bags. Besides that, there is a clash of tastes based on generation and social class: no one wants the Adrienne Vittadini or Coach purse. They want what LeAnn Rimes and Britney Spears carry these days. More sparkle, more glitz, more youth. Violet takes a Ralph Lauren backpack to be polite, but I can tell it's not her style. I ask the girls about their boyfriends and where they are from. They don't say much, but Carolyn, whose boyfriend is locked up in Juvie tells me of her plans to open a Nail Shack. She holds out her own manicure as proof of her expertise and I admire her orange fingernails and wish her luck in this venture. Carolyn has a toddler that her mother is raising just as Violet's two-year-old is being raised by his paternal grandmother. Cheyenne, whose big blond hair seems too large for the rest of her body, whispers to Violet at one point, "Why don't you tell that lady to get her own baby?"

"It's cool," Violet replies. "This is her baby. Let it go, Cheyenne."

"But he's part of you," Cheyenne says, louder, glancing my way.

"I know it," Violet adds, putting her arm around her friend, "I know it."

I gather up the purses no one wants and place grocery money for Violet on the kitchen counter. (This is legal in open adoption.) "Hey, don't leave," Violet says. "Did someone hurt your feelings?"

"No, no," I respond. "I need to get home and grade some papers." These girls remind me of the fourteen-year-old high school freshmen I used to teach. But Carolyn, Cheyenne, and Violet have all dropped out of classes. They look hard and soft at the same time; too much eyeliner and fingernail polish and too little guidance from someone, anyone. Violet recognizes the considerable odds against them and herself. "What right do they have to judge me?" she later asks.

Nor can I judge Violet, no matter what she decides to do. Had I been a mother at nineteen, I could have no more cared for a needy puppy than a child. Faced with an unplanned pregnancy and no income, I would never for a minute have thought of carrying a baby to term and planning an adoption as Violet was in the process of doing. "I don't believe in abortion," Violet tells me thoughtfully one day. "That's just wrong." She hands me a tiny photo album of the baby's first ultrasound pictures tied with a red ribbon. "Happy Valentine's," she adds with a smile. "It's kind of scary if you've never seen these pictures before," she warns. "The baby looks kind of like a Martian at this point, but it's all normal." There is nothing about this process that seems normal to me, least of all the embryonic dream that floats within this tiny piece of celluloid.

In the remaining four months of her pregnancy, Violet and I spend at least three days a week together and talk on the phone frequently. We eat at Sonic, that twenty-first-century drive-in, drinking Dr. Pepper and eating cheddar fries. Thumbing through pages of the *National Enquirer*, we speculate on the lives of the rich and famous. "I'd sure dress better than that if I had her money," Violet says one day, pointing to a particularly trashy-looking Britney Spears. I couldn't agree more. We drive the untidy streets of Sulphur, where houses with tin roofs and porches have rusted and buckled and the only gesture toward curb appeal in this low-rent district are a few yards where someone has taken the trouble to plant pink petunias in old tires. Violet is as knowledgeable as any small-town tour guide, and she narrates the known history of Sulphur's inhabitants. "J.J.

has a meth lab there," she says, pointing to a hollow-looking trailer lodged sideways between two houses, "and that's where a preacher who tried to help me lives." She points up to a cottage where a chalky blue Cadillac sits in the gravel driveway. "That's where Shawnda stays. She gave up a baby for adoption a long time ago."

Other days when I come to visit, we make trips to the Sulphur K-Mart, standing mute before an assortment of baby accoutrements: plastic bathtubs, cribs, strollers. As an experienced mother with a two-year-old, Violet, at age nineteen, is in a position to give me advice on the care and feeding of newborns, a subject on which my forty years of life experience are no help at all. One particular afternoon, we encounter a pregnant fifteen-year-old named Heather, who has run away from home and taken up with Violet's sixteen-year-old drug-dealing brother. She is wearing an oversized black t-shirt advertising the name of a heavy metal band. Heather eyes us some distance away from the baby department, hands on her hips. "I need to talk to you Violet," she says, ignoring me. She flips her waist-length brown hair behind her back with teenage-girl attitude: "It's important."

Violet excuses herself and the two discernibly pregnant girls do several slow laps around the store. In a serious tête-à-tête, they walk the aisles of women's clothing, toys, and automotive equipment, passing me repeatedly as they discuss something that appears to be more than your average teenage trouble. I feel absurd waiting there among baby bottles, diapers, and pacifiers that I cannot believe I will ever have use for. It occurs to me that Heather and Violet should be at a skating rink or a shopping mall gossiping about fashion or boy crushes. They should not be pregnant at the K-Mart in Sulphur, Oklahoma. They should not have boyfriends in trouble with the law. They should have mothers in SUVs who pick them up from cheerleading practice and gymnastics, fathers who coach them for college entrance exams.

When Violet returns she is crying. It turns out her brother is in jail. "I was going to take you to meet him today," she says. "Why does he have to be such a goddamn meth-head?" Later we drive past a rusted trailer where her brother's pit bull is tied up and barking in the mud in front of the mobile home. Violet knocks on the door to no response, and returns sobbing. She does not say anything for a long time. Finally she suggests, "Let's go see Uncle Pig." She cheers herself with this thought and we head up the potholed streets of Sulphur until we come to a tiny, grey-splintered shack at the top of a hill.

"Let's pinch our cheeks and say hello," Violet says as she presses her fingers to her face and bounds out of the car. It turns out that Uncle Pig raised Violet. While her mother was out drunk for weeks or months on end, Violet lived with this gentle relative. "Why do you call him Uncle Pig?" I ask, stepping up the disintegrating sidewalk to his house. "It's because he has some kind of pigmentation on his hand. When I was a little girl they called me Grunt, and I named him Uncle Pig." Violet pulls a greeting card out of her purse for her uncle. "One with mostly pictures," she whispers, "since Uncle Pig can't read."

A tall, thin man with no teeth comes to the door and smiles shyly. I like him instantly. The inside of his house resembles a Walker Evans photograph. Magazine pictures, tacked to the cracked plaster, form haphazard wallpaper. Uncle Pig says, "Hello ma'am," and then proceeds to focus on his favorite niece. "This is the lady; it's her husband and this lady who is going to adopt the baby," Violet tells him in a voice laced with shame. The uncle acknowledges me again, smiles, but turns his attention back to Violet and waits, as if she is the translator and I am a stranger from a distant country.

We sit in the little room on a shabby couch with exposed foam cushions while a mini TV with an aluminum-foil antenna brings in *One Life to Live*. Despite the bad reception, I make out a scene where a middle-class couple converse about the heartbreak of infertility. They hug one another with exaggerated soap-star tenderness, contemplating a childless future or the possibility of adoption.

Once a month, Violet and I visit the OB-GYN together, viewing new ultrasound pictures and asking questions of the doctor. "Look, he's waving to us," Violet says one day, her enormous belly a gel-covered planet. The ultrasound pictures reveal a sweet infant's face, a tiny hand raised in an Okie hello. I want to lift my hand to his, say *see you soon* or something like that, but I am cautious. I have worked hard to practice distance, despite Violet's insistence that she will go through with this. To make myself brave, I read about famous childless women who made plenty of their lives without babies, women who wanted children but found other ways to live remarkably and fully in their absence. Women like Rosa Parks, who became the mother of the civil rights movement while she waited for a baby but none came along. I practice at the role of supporter, telling myself that my job is to help Violet make a decision that she can live with no matter what that decision turns out to be. I say *hers, not mine* when I stare at the ultrasound pictures. I say *hers, not mine* when Violet urges me to feel the baby kicking. I say *hers, not mine* when her teenage friends stare at me with contempt.

One day after an ultrasound appointment, Violet turns to me in the car and asks, "What are you guys gonna name him?" It is four weeks before Mother's Day, a holiday that has caused me some grief in recent years. I feel obliged to reply, "He's not our baby to name yet, Violet. You have every right to change your mind."

She looks sadly out the passenger window. "I'm not gonna change my mind." Turning back, she tries again: "Just tell me. What names do you like?" Finally I give in. I say, "Carson. We like Carson."

As we drive along, Violet's hair whips out the window, a shiny brown flag. In a high-pitched teenage-girl squeal, she wags a playful finger at the dashboard, trying the name out. *"Stop that Carson! Put that down Carson! Come back here Carson!"*

"Do you like it?"

"Sure I like it," she grins, "but you're the one who's gonna be yelling it for the next twenty years."

Weeks later, I go to the mailbox and find a large card in a blue envelope. On the front there are baby's footprints, and inside it reads *Happy Mother's Day. See you soon Mom! Love ya, Carson.* It is signed, swirls and twirls, in Violet's hand.

Despite the overwhelming sincerity of this gesture, I fully expect Violet to change her mind when the labor pains begin. I am not at all shocked on the evening when she calls us to come to the hospital that she does not seem glad to see me for the first time in four months. I have expected it and have tried to practice saying, "It's okay. You can keep him." As though it were up to me. As though I had any right to grant permission.

When Frank and I arrive in the small birthing room with yellow duckling wallpaper, Violet is crying. Her Aunt Crickett and Dusty stand on either side of the bed, each holding one of her hands. Until now, she and this infant have lived in the same private province. Now she knows that this baby might move away for good. Violet has a Good Samaritan's heart, a sweet disposition, so her confusion comes as no surprise.

"How will I ever forget him?" she whispers to her aunt.

"You won't ever forget him," Crickett says.

Suddenly the labor pain starts again, and I see that childbirth is no picnic, even for a nineteen-year-old.

"I love you Violet," I blurt out, helpless and guilty, rubbing her toes.

"You better," she gasps as she manages to grin at me, "cause this hurts."

I have seen babies born on television but never in real life. At last Carson emerges, screaming and wriggling, a red, angry infant. Violet holds him first, tears running down her cheeks, then hands him to the nurse who hands him to me for a moment

Carson Kates

and then to Frank. He weighs five pounds. Dusty, who has massaged Violet's legs and coached her throughout the birth, is visibly upset. Although there has been some question from the beginning about who the biological father might be, Dusty has always believed he's the one. He looks at Frank and pulls a ball cap awkwardly toward his face to hide the fact he is crying. "Send that boy to college," he says softly. Then he walks out of the room.

All night long Frank begins a love affair in front of the window of the hospital nursery, making ridiculous enamored father gestures, tapping his fingers lightly on the glass. Down the hall, Violet is sick as a dog from the pain medicine, and I stand beside her bed holding a pan while she vomits again and again. The nurses are baffled by our situation. They look at me with eyes that say *baby stealer* and I think maybe I am. Maybe blood trumps everything; maybe there is no reason in the world why we should be given this child.

In the morning Violet asks to hold him. I take pictures of the tiny girl and tinier infant. "That flash is gonna hurt his little eyes," she says, her hand slanting like a tent above his face. She is in tears, and for a long time does not speak. They look so *Madonna-and-child*-like. I am a third wheel. I wait for Violet to look at me and say, "I can't do this," but after a few minutes she hands the baby to the nurse and returns to her room to gather her things. Before she can be legally released from the hospital, she walks out the door. Her cousin Donel comes to pick her up. I walk with them out into the harsh Oklahoma sunlight spilling over the parking lot. She is no longer crying, but I cannot stop. Hugging me before she gets in the car, Violet instructs resolutely: "Go in there and show off your new baby." Then she slams the door on her cousin's red Chevrolet and drives away.

In the weeks that follow, Violet signs away her parental rights to Carson. She and Dusty split up, and he goes to live with his emphysemic mother, who is raising Violet and Dusty's first child, near Sulphur. Every few months Violet calls to check on Carson, but I hear through Crickett and her cousin that she deeply regrets her decision, that she has begun a descent into drugs and nomadic stops around the state. For a long time no one knows where she is, and I feel responsible for her trouble.

Crickett calls one day to tell me that Violet is living with a meth dealer in Shawnee, Oklahoma, who is twenty years her senior, a man with a long prison record and head-to-toe tattoos. She has told her aunt that she might be pregnant again. But a few days later when Crickett goes to fetch her at the man's house, he tells her that Violet has taken her things and gone.

No matter how I turn it over in my head, I am implicated in the accumulated heartbreak that is Violet's life. I try to assuage my guilt by imagining that one day Violet and I might stand together arm in arm at Carson's high school graduation, basking in some kind of collaborative motherhood. Crickett assures me that this will never be the case. She tells me that her niece has done the right thing, but she will need to move on. I know the value of what Violet has lost and what I have gained. This child is an every morning Christmas. He opens his mouth like a baby bird, searching for a bottle with his tiny lips. Relatives fly in to see him and celebrate him. We are given multiple baby showers that Carson attends, oblivious to the car seats and strollers unwrapped in his midst. Frank and I go to court, and in a ceremony that resembles marriage, we raise our right hands and pledge to take care of him, to feed him, clothe him, love him. Then we are given a birth certificate with his name changed to ours, and that is supposed to be that.

I buy a scrapbook with a blue pastel elephant on the front and place Carson's wristband from the hospital and first pictures in it. I wrestle with how to tell this story. It seems a lie to omit photos of Violet, Dusty, and the other relatives on the birth side of his family. But for the time being, I put those pictures in a box in our closet, and make our narrative more traditional despite my instinct to do otherwise.

Months pass, but one day near Carson's first birthday, Violet calls to ask me to pick her up in Shawnee and drive her to Sulphur. She gives me directions to a ramshackle house, grey paint peeling from the wood. No longer the all-American-looking girl in the polka-dot maternity clothes she used to wear, Violet sports the baggy shirt and jeans of a rap artist. Her small hands wave as she talks, an array of gold and silver rings on every finger. "I'm writing songs now; I'm going to become a drummer," she asserts with determination. Gothic blue glitter polish dots her tiny fingernails. I hand Carson to her when we stop to eat and she carries him into the diner. "What a chunk," she says, pinching his cheeks. "How much do you weigh, little man?"

Inside the restaurant, I put Carson in the highchair at the end of the table. I see that there are needle marks, bruised moons that dot the inside of Violet's arms. "Well," she says with adolescent indifference, "I guess you know I'm on drugs." It turns out that *on drugs* means Crank, that toxic methamphetamine that is cheap and easy to make.

A waitress approaches our table, puts water down before us. "Whose baby?" she asks, assuming it is not a trick question. She is a waitress, I tell myself, not King Solomon, but inquiry hangs in the air: Who is the *real* mother? We pause nervously. "He's ours," I say, smiling. But then I get a strange look from the waitress, who has concluded we are lesbians. I gesture toward Violet. "She gave birth to him and allowed my husband and me to adopt him." "Oh . . . " the waitress replies slowly, backing toward the kitchen, sorry to have opened this can of worms.

On the way to Sulphur, Carson sleeps in the back. Out of the blue Violet remarks, "I don't know why I ever gave him up really." She could be speaking these words to a therapist or a stranger, for they do not seem to contain particular resentment toward me. She is simply stating a fact, like *yellow is the color of the sun.* I don't know what to say, so I say nothing. But I am at long last territorial. Making bottles, changing diapers, and walking the floors at night with a sick infant have made me a mother, and as much as I love this woman-child in my car, I do not think Carson would be better off in her care. I am shocked by my internal response, determined as I was not to participate in a dueling moms scenario, but I find I am not above it after all.

When I can no longer wait to go the bathroom, I pull into a dilapidated gas station. We enter the establishment, and I hand Carson to Violet, visiting the ladies' room as quickly as I can. I have visions of her running away with the baby and up to the house of someone who believes in the superiority of biological mothers. What if they are gone when I come out and I never see Carson again? But when I emerge, Violet is feeding Carson little bites of powdered-sugar doughnuts she has purchased from a vending machine. She carries him to the car and we put him in the car seat and drive away. Hours later, she climbs out of the

car and hugs me, then opens the back door, kisses Carson, and
waves goodbye to us from the front porch of a friend's house.

∽

Listening to National Public Radio one morning, I am haunted
by the voices of women whose lives have been devastated by the
adoptive process. They call from Duluth, Denver, and Boston to
speak of babies surrendered thirty years ago, as though it were
yesterday or last week. One is a writer, one a nun, one a farmer's
wife who had other children. But they do not forget. They tell of
being thrust into homes for unwed mothers, denied the opportunity to touch what their own bodies had held and nurtured
for nine months. Some were never told the sex of the child. A
few women speak in voices of well-contained despair; others
cry when they talk of children who have not looked for them
or about whom they know nothing. One woman says when the
news reported a case of child abuse in a town where her son's
adoptive parents lived, she tortured herself by wondering, *Is
that my child?*

Adoptees speak of the bureaucracy of failed searches for
birth parents or those that led to deceased parents, and other
genealogical dead ends. They talk about a desire to know. *Who
do I look like? Do I have biological siblings?* A beneficiary of the
adoptive process, I am implicated in the pain of these voices.
I want to rescue Carson and Violet from the heartache these
people describe, but I am not sure some days if keeping in touch
will be more or less painful.

We read stories to Carson about adoption called *How I was
Adopted, Adoption is for Always*, and *Tell Me Again about the
Night I Was Born*. I show Carson pictures of Violet both pregnant and holding him as a baby, and I try to make the term *birth
mother* part of his considerable toddler vocabulary. One day as I
explain to him that I couldn't have a baby so Violet gave birth to
him and allowed us to adopt him, Carson studies her photo and
emergent belly. "She has a nice tummy!" he announces at last. "I
was in there, waving to my mom and dad!"

Violet sends cards to Carson on Valentine's Day, Easter, and Christmas. She writes *I love you and I miss you* and signs them *Violet*. She sends pictures of herself when she was a baby, mementos for a keepsake book. I place these items in a wooden box in the top of our closet to give to him someday. It seems preferable to allowing Carson to think he was abandoned at a hospital without a second thought.

No matter how you come by your children, parenting is a crooked road, full of potholes that leave you panting beside any particular route you are fortunate enough to travel. I spend too much valuable time worried about the future, but I am happy to be jolted out of my thoughts by a four-year-old who needs a peanut butter sandwich or help putting on his Batman suit. On any given day, Carson runs through the house squealing with a delight that is high-pitched and joyful, a voice that is all Violet's. Sometimes it is haunting to have her here, but other times it is a comfort. The fact that she brought him into this world, that he has, in fact, another mother and father, does not diminish Frank or me, does not change the fact that he is our son, the son of all that is in us. People who are curious about adoption always assume we have traveled a long and complicated distance to get our child, and that much is certainly true. But when they ask, "What country does he come from?" I always laugh and say, "Oklahoma Country!"

This afternoon, from the backseat of the station wagon, Carson asks me to put on his CD of nursery rhymes. He waves his arm out the window, keeping time with "The Farmer in the Dell." He is jacked up on the sugar cookies he ate before we set off for the playground, wisps of his blond hair moving in the wind like so much dandelion fuzz. He is wearing black cowboy boots, red shorts, and a Spiderman t-shirt.

It is easy to live in moments of such perfection. I park the car and lift the little cowboy from his seat. There's no telling what the future holds, but as I take his small hand and walk toward the park, I know I can live with this story. I feel a great affection for Carson's biological relatives who are knitted into the how and why of this boy. But before I can think too much about it, I am interrupted by Carson's insistent voice. "Push me Mama!" he yells as he runs up to the swing set and takes a seat. I watch as he begins to pump determinedly, stretching his feet toward the white clouds. "Push me hard as you can," he adds, gliding back and forth, back and forth. "I want to get up to the moon."

Cowgirl boots

Great Plains Salvage

⟳

Whenever I'm in a bad mood or don't know what to do about a problem I have, I get in the car and go straight away to look at junk. Some people might call what I do "antiquing," but that is too genteel a word for scavenger hunts in dusty, rusty establishments called Bill's Used Furniture or the Chickasha Salvage Yard. There is something about searching through shelves of objects that no one wants anymore for something you don't particularly need that momentarily cures obsessive worry and PMS.

Oklahoma junk stores boast wares that are distinctly regional: Covered-wagon cookie jars, drinking glasses with trite images of Indians, and boxes of old lizard-skin cowgirl boots. Also plentiful are lamps with oil-derrick bases, ashtrays with the names of petroleum companies, and other oil boom decor. I once bought a sterling-silver oil derrick for my charm bracelet because the oil wells of Oklahoma are beloved to me; they remind me of something my son said when he was two years old. Shortly after we returned from France, Carson looked out the

car window and saw a tall, wrought-iron, open-latticed oil plat-
form looming on the horizon. "Look, Mommy," he yelled, "it's
the Eiffel Tower!" The day I had the oil derrick soldered to my
charm bracelet was a day I promised myself never to forget my
son's remark or the oil rig silhouettes across Oklahoma's pastel
skies.

Friends point out to me that I could get many of the items
I have collected over the years much cheaper at garage sales.
Thanks, but no thanks: there is a world of difference between
a garage sale and a junk store. Junk store owners take the time
to amass a mélange of miscellany far more interesting than one
family's castaways scattered the length of a driveway. When was
the last time you saw equestrian gear in a garage sale? Though
I have never been in the market for bridles or stirrups, I enjoy
running my fingers over the leather-tooled name of Matilda on
a custom-made saddle. *Who is Matilda?* I wonder. *Is she or was
she a real cowgirl?*

I am, I confess, a plaything of fashion and thus a sucker for
vintage print dresses and skirts from the forties or fifties. Particularly appealing to me are garments decorated with rickrack,
the zigzag ribbon that graces the hemlines of numerous skirts
and blouses of different eras. Fabric companies now reproduce
vintage designs and fashions at exorbitant prices; most of the
clothes I have purchased cost less than twenty dollars apiece.
If I had the time and space, I would love to curate a clothing
museum, but for now that museum is my overcrowded closet.
My clothing hunts reveal that the women of Oklahoma in other
times were like women everywhere who succumb to the forces
of trends. I am the proud owner of a spring-green dress of dot-
ted Swiss from the 1940s and a turquoise gingham sundress
from the 1950s with red rickrack. It is not just the design and
the condition of the garment that attract me; I am always curious about the woman who owned the item. Does she still live
in Oklahoma? Did she wear the romper to the soda shop or
barbeque? Was she a blond or a brunette? How did the garment

travel out of her closet and into my hands? Was this a favorite item, one discarded at long last because of age or weight gain? Or an unwanted gift that didn't suit the owner's tastes?

In addition to acquiring a significant clothing collection over the years, I have also amassed a number of tooled leather purses imprinted with flowers, cacti, horses, or other western insignia. These items became fashionable in this part of the country in the mid-twentieth century. I wear them with various pairs of cowgirl boots that take up ample space in my closet. The truth is I am a sucker for boots my size in shades of brown and red that have been tossed away by another owner. I am a girl who won't get near a horse, let alone ride one, but it makes sense somehow to stock up on boots in case I need them.

Junk store owners will congratulate you when you choose something they have held in high esteem, though they are sad at some level to see the object go. They will look at you fondly when you carry the yellow chenille bedspread with a cactus emblem to the register and they will tell you some story about how they acquired the piece from a female cousin of the governor or the ex-wife of Thomas Stafford, Oklahoma astronaut. Some owners move so little merchandise that you wonder how they make a living. Many of them call to mind an image of Steinbeck's Muley Graves, making a last stand in the ghost towns of Oklahoma. Thrift store vendors have shored up pieces of history from the town and the surrounding area. Propped up as one of the few commercial holdouts of otherwise deserted locales, they remain stubbornly open for business.

Webster's dictionary defines junk as "1: Old iron, glass, or paper, or waste; *also*: discarded articles, 2: a shoddy product." This is a shoddy definition, in my opinion, for what junk is. Junk is a potential treasure to be discovered among other items like an olive telephone from the seventies or someone's throwaway fuchsia Barney doll. When you take the item home and place it on a shelf or a coffee table in isolation from more pedestrian objects, its value emerges. The beauty and the challenge lie in the ability to see what the object will become in another context.

Take the embroidered picture of two ponies I discovered in a Goodwill store. Though a small stain bleeds up from the corner on this particular piece of embroidery, the ponies are unharmed, stitched in lovely light browns and mint greens. On the back is a hand-signed dedication on cardboard: *To Elmer from Nadine. Happy Birthday, 1949.* Who is Elmer? Who is Nadine? Why did she embroider horses for him? These seem to me crucial questions on the morning that I discover this piece of handiwork. I am delighted to find, months later, in another Goodwill store a hundred miles from the other, a similar set of horses stitched in the same mint green and light brown, this one with a giant horseshoe background. Today the set of pony pictures hangs in Carson's room, as fine an example of western tapestry as you will see anywhere.

Another regional ware that I appreciate is pottery bearing the stamp of Frankoma. It was not love at first sight; some of the Frankoma colors are simply hideous, reminiscent of the harvest gold or sunset orange palate of 1970s living rooms and kitchens. When I first came across a few Frankoma items, I thought they were ugly, and I would pass over them any day for a piece of McCoy or Hull—bigger names on the pottery collector's spectrum. I was impressed, however, to learn that at one time Frankoma mugs, pitchers, and other utilitarian ware had graced many homes in the Sooner State, blending aesthetic form with function. The pottery firm was founded by John Frank, a one-time ceramics professor at the University of Oklahoma. He left academic life, however, to found a business that made use of indigenous clay. His wife suggested that he pair his name with the last part of *Oklahoma*, and voilà: Frankoma Pottery was born.

The loveliest Frankoma glaze, in my opinion, is Prairie Green. This color became increasingly valuable when Martha Stewart ran a story on it in her magazine several years ago before her stock market debacle. The green is a faded, southwestern

Wagon

tone, tinted at times with a brown enamel edge. It is a color that makes me supremely happy, and that is why I have filled shelves throughout our house with some sixty-odd pieces of it: a water pitcher in the shape of a wagon wheel; a plate that commemorates pioneer women and the state flag, and many other ceramic eccentricities that say *Oklahoma*.

One of John Frank's daughters tells the story of how her father, a deeply religious man, traveled to various small towns in Oklahoma to give talks to the Kiwanis or other rotary groups eager for tales of his success. Frank would stand in front of the group with a potter's wheel, working the clay, shaping a narrative that was two parts Horatio Alger and three parts Baptist testimony. Telling the story of his business, he would finish the pot as he spoke humbly, explaining that he could not take credit for achievement that he owed to a higher being. "I am," he professed, "merely clay in the Master's hands."

Regional wares like my beloved Frankoma pottery are often housed in dingy buildings in jalopy towns across the prairie. Trace your fingers around an atlas, over small towns named Cahill, Hugo, or Anadarko, and you will find no lovelier lexicon of named places. Tishomingo, Wewoka, and Broken Bow are other cartographic jewels that lie across the sparsely populated state. Unfortunately the towns that roll so easily off your tongue are not so easy on your eyes. Main Street after Main Street across Oklahoma is run down, in disrepair. I might have failed to see what beauty there is in dilapidated buildings that are sad versions of their former glory had I not viewed a photography exhibit by John Margolies twenty years ago called "Vanishing Architecture in America." This show presented color photographs of colossal cowboy-boot snack bars, motor courts themed in Alamo or sombrero facades, and other vernacular folk architecture of the American roadside.

I have also gained a new perspective on the buildings constructed to draw consumers off various highways, including the famous Route 66 stretching across the American West. Until the first Holiday Inns and Golden Arches began to appear in the early 1950s, there was no standardized roadside architecture apart from service stations in America. The mom-and-pop joints were built locally and had regional charm. As time passed and chain restaurants like Denney's and Stuckey's became the mode of the day on highway interchanges, these original structures began to look crude by comparison.

When I first came across photographs by Margolies, Quinta Scott, and others who had captured thematic vernacular architecture of an era, I longed to see the buildings in any form they still existed. Imagine my delight when I arrived in Oklahoma and saw that it was an architectural historian's dream. Numerous abandoned service stations with canopies and rusted antique gas pumps stand along highways. Old motor courts and diners are still in business in towns like El Reno and Anadarko. Best of all, the kitschy neon signs remain. Some diners and motels combine the stucco facades in the tradition of the Alamo with glass-blocked windows and elements of the Streamline Moderne in an interesting collision of architectural styles.

Such architecture is now part of my lived experience. I am happy that nearly defunct roadside diners and filling stations hang on in the kinds of buildings that have long been torn down in other states. Although the paint is often peeling and the old signs that say CAFÉ hang crooked in the wind, they are still vibrant. Like the junk in stores I frequent, they are pieces of history.

It is a thrill to exit a salvage warehouse with a treasure in your hand and enter a nearby local diner that would have long ago been razed for a McDonalds or a Burger King were the building elsewhere. The Liberty Drug Store in Chickasha is one such place. It boasts an authentic soda fountain and nickel coffee. One day Carson and I emerge from a dark and damp rummage house, blinking our eyes in the Main Street sunlight. "Refreshment time!" Carson declares with his latest treasure—an empty toy gun holster from the fifties—tucked under his arm. We head into Liberty and order him a milkshake made with vintage equipment and, for me, a cup of nickel coffee.

There was a time when every town had an old-fashioned soda fountain like the one in the Liberty Drug Store with its marble-top counter, massive mirror backdrop, and gleaming metal. There are sloping glass cases filled with candies and chocolates enough to delight any child. Carson and I choose

two of the stainless-steel stools and order up. In no time coffee
and a frosty treasure are set before us. My son doesn't know that
these places, or small valuables like his toy holster, are infre-
quent finds. It's just another good junking day in Oklahoma as
far as he's concerned.

∽

I have amassed a collection of junk in the last decade that has
taken over my house and the largest storage unit one can rent
in Norman. I simply have no more room for hoarding objects.
Ironically, I am a minimalist at heart; I prefer rooms with more
space and fewer things. In my living room *less is more.* However,
when I am out shopping, *more is more.* Keep in mind that I
am a serious claustrophobe and you will better understand my
predicament. On the one hand, I have a compulsion to buy old
stuff; on the other hand, I need open space for my sanity. Go
figure. These are the contradictions of my psyche that I wish I
could treat with medication or a larger storage unit.

It is bad enough that I cannot stop collecting junk; the greater
tragedy is that I seem to have passed this compulsion on to my
son. The other day I went to drop off a bag of old clothing at the
Salvation Army drive-thru bin. Carson napped in the back seat.
He awakened as I tossed the bag into the box. "Is that my reindeer sweater?" he said anxiously as he spied the red sleeve of a
Christmas sweater two sizes too small for him popping out of
the bag. "It doesn't fit you anymore," I told him as I pulled away.

"I love that sweater and now I'll never see it again!" he cried,
rubbing his eyes. "I wanted to keep it in my drawer and remember the times when I was a little boy."

"You're still a little boy," I reminded him. "Young enough to
own a reindeer sweater that fits you. I'll buy you another one."

"I want that one," he sobbed, broken-hearted.

I tried to comfort him as we drove away. The truth is, I knew
just how he felt. I could only hope that Carson might grow
out of this phase and not become a full-fledged seeker of junk,
addicted to hanging out in scrappy places looking for items that

will be hard to turn loose of someday or forever. I pulled into the Snow Cone Hut parking lot, hoping to bribe away my son's tears with flavored ice. I comforted myself with the thought that one could do worse than become a collector of other people's castaways. While roadside architecture might be in danger of vanishing, there seem to be a lot of chuck-wagon dishes and ranch tools left. As long as we live in Oklahoma, it is a pretty safe bet that we will never run out of places to buy junk, even if we run out of places to put it.

Miss Dorrie

Miss Dorrie at Big Sky

In New York and California, thematic daycare is all the rage. If you have the money and the patience for a marathon application process, you may earn your child a seat in a bilingual school where the teachers speak German or Mandarin. Incoming two-year-olds are guaranteed to master two languages by the time they are five. If languages aren't your concern, enroll your son or daughter in a natural foods daycare where every meal and snack served to children is organic and that devil sugar is sternly outlawed. Perhaps you prefer a musical outlet for your child: choose then a center where boys and girls learn piano or violin and how to discern Beethoven from Mozart by age four.

I don't know when specialized nursery schools first arrived on the coasts, but in Norman, Oklahoma, the only thematic school options are of a religious nature, and the Savior is the name of their game. Many of our daycare centers have names like *Pentecostal Family Holiness School* and *Preach Unto Them Jesus Academy*. My colleagues and I lament that we have none of the exotic coastal preschool alternatives on the central plains.

On the other hand, I am relieved that I do not have to attend a workshop to learn how to write an application essay for entrance into a preschool whose status will one day ensure my child's acceptance into the Ivy Leagues.

In the fall of every year, Manhattan residents face a Darwinian admissions process for the "best" private nursery schools. There are 15 applicants for every slot. This is more competitive than Harvard—which only has 11 applications for every opening. It seems ludicrous that some parents, desperate to remain in New York City, are faced with the daunting prospect of endowing the preschool with a $20,000 gift while paying tuition each year to the tune of another $20,000!

While there are no gourmet daycare centers in our vicinity offering organic lunches or intensive study in one or more languages, we do have a few master artist teachers of our own. One of them is Miss Dorrie Trent of the Big Sky Learning Center.

Miss Dorrie is a fifty-year-old hippie who wears t-shirts with environmentally friendly sayings like *Earth First* and *Good Planets are Hard to Find*. Her long curly hair is always in a bun, except when she takes it down to dance wildly like Isadora Duncan in a room of four-year-olds. She is a beekeeper, and, rumor has it, a former boxer.

Children have discriminating taste in teachers; Carson would no more pledge allegiance to a subpar caregiver than he would to a cartoon show that insults his considerable intelligence. If it weren't for Miss Dorrie's extensive knowledge of dinosaurs, Carson might never have given her the time of day. On the first morning we enter the Bison classroom (all the student groups at Big Sky are named for Oklahoma animals and plants), Carson announces dishonestly to Miss Dorrie that he is on his way to the dinosaur museum and *not* to school.

Miss Dorrie eyes him ferociously then shakes her wild hair out of the bun and tosses it in front of her face. "Have you ever seen a woolly mammoth?" she asks. From his coat pocket Carson produces his own plastic version of the prehistoric animal and makes a little roar as he holds it to her face, but his display is nothing in comparison to the imitation of the extinct species that Miss Dorrie unleashes. The eccentric teacher stomps around the room with her arms braided together in a trunk and her unruly mane of hair shaking over that trunk for the desired effect. Carson squeals with delight as he and Dorrie bond over woolly mammoths, and I am free to leave without incident.

The path of motherhood is paved with guilt. My conscience chides me for everything from giving Carson insufficient quantities of vegetables to leaving him in someone else's care while I go out to earn the almighty buck. When you imagine a disastrous cause-effect relationship between your every move and the future neurosis of your child, you need someone like Miss Dorrie to make you feel that not only will your son be alive when you return, but he might come home knowing a thing or two about Mars or the various species of sharks.

One snowy day when remorse drives me back to the center early to fetch Carson, I find the Bisons gathered at the top of a small hill outside the school. With an array of cardboard bobsleds and skis fashioned by Miss Dorrie, the children are holding a Winter Olympics. Their ecstasy is evident from the parking lot. From some distance, I see Carson jumping up and down, begging to be the next person down the hill. And so I return to work and leave him to Miss Dorrie. Later, in the classroom, all the Bisons are pronounced winners and medals are placed around each of their necks while "The Star-Spangled Banner" plays on a tape recorder. "We won!" one child announces to me as I enter the room. "Can you believe it? We all won the Olympics!" The children continue to wear the medals to school for weeks after this event, and Carson still sports his ketchup-stained ribbon around the house whenever the mood strikes him.

During the Chinese New Year, a lengthy orange dragon hangs from the ceiling of the classroom and winds its way all around and above the preschoolers. Miss Dorrie wears a satin

red kimono, her long hair in a braid down her back. She provides the children a traditional Asian dish: a sweet rice ball
brewed in a soup. Aside from a few of the pickier eaters in the
class, most of the children try the soup and pronounce it deli-
cious. Because it is the fifteenth day of the Chinese New Year
and this day is usually celebrated as the lantern festival, the children make their own lanterns out of square cardboard milk car-
tons and red-and-yellow construction paper. Later they have a
parade around the playground and the rest of Big Sky Learning
Center.

Regardless of the holiday season at hand, entering Miss Dorrie's classroom is a marvelous visual experience. Like other preschool rooms, it is subdivided into "centers" for art, writing,
books, blocks, science, and dramatic play. The walls are decorated with the children's crayoned self-portraits and abstract
finger paintings. Cardboard whales, squids, and other sea creatures in primary colors hang from the ceiling. But Miss Dorrie
takes pedagogical risks that might be strictly outlawed in Manhattan or the Bay Area.

Take, for example, the work stand with nails partially driven
into a deep piece of wood. At this station, kids are allowed to
use real (yes, real) hammers and screwdrivers! You might be
surprised to hear that to this day, no child has taken to using a
hammer or a screwdriver on classmates. The kids wear swim-
ming masks as protective eyewear, and construction worker
hats as they pound away, two at a time, in this work space. As
you might imagine, this station is a favorite among the children,
but could you hear the parental outrage if they tried this at the
92nd Street Y?

In a more "elite" nursery school, children might be denied
one of the most extraordinary experiences of the year: a les-
son on beekeeping. I enter the classroom one day to find Miss
Dorrie standing before twenty Bison children in a suit that
resembles an astronaut's. Next to her is a locked beehive flat,
with thousands of bees scooting beneath the glass in silent
frenzy. I cannot help thinking that this scene would not play

in Manhattan, ripe as it might be for a lawsuit. But Miss Dorrie takes the children outside and lines them up against a wall. Following a caveat about why only grown-ups should use lighters, she lights a smoker and then in a grand pedagogic gesture, she hands the manual bellows of her beekeeping instrument to four-year-old Carson and allows him to pump smoke out like a magic genie from a bottle.

"What do bees do when smoke comes toward the hive?" Miss Dorrie asks from her astro-bee suit, no doubt sweating beyond belief in the ninety-degree temperatures. "They rush to protect the queen!" yells Will, his lips stained dark with grape juice.

"One hundred percent correct!" Miss Dorrie answers, motioning a gloved thumbs-up sign to the child, the enthusiasm for both her bees and her children unruffled by the stifling heat.

On another day Riley brings to school a small garter snake that her mother found in the yard. Children take turns handling it, and they even let it slither through the reading area for a while. When the snake has to go back in the shoe box, Miss Dorrie asks the children to wash their hands, and the day progresses without incident. No one has to sign a permission slip releasing Big Sky from suit or responsibility in the event that someone contracts reptile-induced dermatitis.

Sometimes the Bisons have a picnic lunch under the trees in front of the school. They eat standard fare: baloney and cheese, carrot sticks, the occasional Pop Tart (no organic pita pocket laced with avocado and topped with cugurt sauce or fair-trade banana chips here!). Miss Dorrie points out birds and other animals and insects that cross their path. When they are finished eating, they fill a nature bag with pinecones, stones, and sticks. I know that New Yorkers have Central Park, but I am glad there are big trees in front of Big Sky that my son can walk to without the interference of honking horns and traffic. I am happy he can pick up a pinecone or a blue jay's feather right outside his classroom beneath prairie clouds that lift high above Big Sky Learning Center.

Parents of the Bison children know that Miss Dorrie is extraordinary. We stand around at birthday parties, singing her praises, knowing that next year's Kindergarten teachers will pale by comparison. "I think we'll all be disappointed," one mother comments sadly as she bounces a baby on her knees. "How can anyone measure up to Miss Dorrie?" I am certain that her salary is much too low for the commitment and intelligence she brings to the job. America invests an enormous amount of faith in the idea of education, but not much in teachers. Miss Dorrie calls to mind legendary pedagogical geniuses like Mary Poppins, who enter children's lives with mystical tour de force.

And pity the poor substitute. One day a much younger woman with a perky sorority-girl smile takes Miss Dorrie's place for the afternoon. She is a chipper blond girl with a week's worth of craft ideas in her backpack. From the get-go, the children can't help but let her know she doesn't get it. When the young woman calls the kids to tables to work on a pinecone bird feeder project, Hallie announces, "We don't do crafts at this time of the day. It's group time," she says, pointing to a chart on the wall.

Miss Tiffany looks disappointed for a moment but then breaks out her smile and calls them all into group. "Let's sing the 'Itsy Bitsy Spider' song."

"We don't do *that* song," Lee says. "That song is for babies. Do you know 'The Dog Upset the Apple Cart?'"

The expression on Miss Tiffany's face reveals that indeed she does not. But then she again brightens: "Bison children, I want to teach you a new word today. It's called *flexible*. Flexible means going with the flow, being able to break with routine a little bit. Let's all say this word three times."

The group of children chimes in like a choir and repeats after Miss Tiffany: "*Flexible, flexible, flexible.*"

"Very good," Miss Tiffany pronounces. "Now can someone please come up here and give us the weather report?"

Allison raises her hand.

"Miss Flexible, we don't do the weather that way!"

Experiences such as this have taught the children that the Miss Dorries of the world are few and far between. They are protective of their teacher to the point of impinging on her freedom when they think it necessary. One morning when I arrive with Carson, the children are already on the carpet for story time. Miss Dorrie holds a book in her hand, but she stops to remark that the next day is her birthday and she won't be at school. Cole raises his hand and asks inquisitively, "How old are you Miss Dorrie?"

"Tomorrow I will be fifty-one years old."

There is immediate weeping from one child in the classroom audience.

"What is the matter, Ashley?" Dorrie tilts her head, puzzled by the sudden outburst.

"Oh Miss Dorrie," the distraught child replies, "tomorrow you're going to be dead!"

"No! No! No!" Dorrie explains compassionately, but firmly. "I am not going to be dead! I am taking a holiday for my birthday." But it is too late to calm the concern that has rippled through the Bison entourage. The children insist that Miss Dorrie must call in on her day off to let the children know she is still alive.

While she is gone the children paint a banner that says HAPPY BIRTHDAY MISS DORRIE and they sign their names on it. She confesses to me later that she kept the banner up in her house for two months, until her husband forced her to take it down and put it in the attic along with twenty years' worth of art from other children. "I can't bear to throw it away," she says to me one day on the playground as we stand watching twenty-four kids unleash their considerable energy on tire swings, sandboxes, and sliding boards. Children run up to give her brief sound bites of information. "Look at this dinosaur tooth I found, Miss Dorrie," Jane says, holding up a small piece of gravel.

"Do you think it's from a T-Rex?" Miss Dorrie asks in a gravely serious voice.

"Most definitely," the child replies, as she gallops off to collect another.

Another girl skids to a stop in front of us.

"Miss Dorrie, my brother's tooth fell out last night."

The teacher's hand covers her mouth in feigned shock.

"Will the tooth fairy visit?"

"Not my brother," the child replies.

You might think that I am simply partial to Miss Dorrie in the ways that parents are partial to any teacher who attends to his or her child with loving care. But recently, a former East Coaster moved to Oklahoma who confirmed for me both the madness of the New Yorker's pursuit of the ultimate nursery school and Miss Dorrie's grandness.

"I'm so relieved to be out of Manhattan," the mother tells me. "We were in one of the finest schools," she explains, "but the competition was overwhelming. It was tough explaining to Michael why he couldn't have a circus for his birthday like his other friends. The lunches and snacks *were* extraordinary. I like it here though," she adds, pushing a strand of hair behind her ear as she watches her son run toward the sandbox. "It's so normal . . ."

I'm not sure what normal is, but I know that teachers like Miss Dorrie are not the usual preschool standard. The Bison children may not speak Mandarin or German; perhaps they cannot tell Beethoven from Mozart. They may eat more sugar than is good for them. But pull one of Miss Dorrie's kids aside and he or she will amaze you with a considerable knowledge of aquatic life and the alphabet. These children are experts on the crucial subjects as far as I'm concerned. All you have to do is ask, and one of them will cup his or her hand to your ear and whisper everything you need to know about dinosaur teeth or the lives of bees.

Dona Kay Rule, barrel racer

Girls in the Ring

◠

The book I loved most as a child was called *Annie Oakley: Little Sure Shot.* I checked it out from the school library at least once a month. I figured if a girl from Ohio could become a mythic figure of the American West, there was hope for me. I wished desperately that I had been born in Montana or New Mexico instead of Ohio. My chances for becoming a cowgirl would have increased substantially were my father a rancher instead of a salesman. However, a frequent fantasy helped me in those days to escape what I believed to be the dull Midwest: turning my backyard into a rodeo arena. The banana seat of my bicycle became the bare back of a galloping horse as I imagined myself shooting a bull's eye; I rode around my yard and suburban Columbus housing development holding part of an old clothesline, trying to lasso invisible cattle and perform pathetic rope tricks. I begged my parents to take me to the Wild, Wild West so that I could see the frontier that fed my childhood imagination by way of television shows like *Bonanza* and *The Big Valley.*

When my parents finally took their eight-year-old would-be cowgirl daughter to the Badlands of South Dakota and to the great prairies that opened out across former Indian Territory, I was thrilled when we made a stop at the Buffalo Bill Historical Museum in Cody, Wyoming. Behind museum glass were the beaded, buckskin cowgirl costumes Annie Oakley wore in Wild West shows while performing such tricks as shooting the ash from her husband's cigarette or an apple from a dog's head. Oakley's outfits were simple but not plain. There were embroidered flowers on the skirts and stitched ribbon along the hems, giving them a distinctly feminine flair. I fantasized about playing Annie Oakley in a film version of her life so that I could wear those costumes or others like them. John Wayne would already be slated to play Buffalo Bill Cody. "We'd love to have you on board, Missy," he might say. Then we'd shake on it and I would join the greatest Wild West show in the land.

For my birthday that year I received a cowgirl outfit featured in the glossy pages of a J.C. Penney catalogue. It was a woodsy-green denim number—a skirt and blouse with mother-of-pearl snaps that ran down the front of the shirt. Two loopy lariats, embroidered in black thread waved just below the collar. I already owned a set of six-shooters with plastic red jewels on each of the black leather holsters. The red stars on my black cowboy boots matched the fake gems on my holster set, and I spent a good deal of time in front of the mirror admiring the entire western ensemble. I would soon learn, however, that it is not enough to love the gear of a cowgirl: *one must be brave and ride a horse.*

This was a challenge for me because during the same summer vacation that I got to eye Oakley's embroidered western wear, I acquired full-blown horse phobia. After nagging my parents for hundreds of miles across the middle section of the United States to let me ride a horse, somewhere in South Dakota I was permitted to climb on a pony named Fireball. My horse quickly galloped away from the trail and ran on to a busy highway and oncoming traffic (I still recall the sounds of honking horns and screeching brakes). Fireball would not stop, and it was some time before the trail guide successfully led my horse and me from the highway. I was terrified of horses after that and through with riding, but nothing dimmed my admiration for the ultimate cowgirl. We had a neighbor who was fond of belittling the accomplishments of notable women. "Women don't shoot guns," he said matter-of-factly. This man told me that Annie Oakley was not really a cowgirl but a circus performer. *Had he seen her boots, guns, and medals in Wyoming?* Perhaps the Wild West shows that employed Oakley and others like her were tented dramas where "cowboys," "Indians," and gun aficionados wowed the crowds, but no one did what she did better than she did it. In 1968, you had to scour history's pages to find strong female role models, so any cowgirl from Ohio was bound to get my attention.

During my *Little Sure Shot* phase, I was a loyal fan of the syndicated TV western *The Big Valley.* Widowed matriarch Victoria Barkley (played by Barbara Stanwick) ruled the considerable estate that was the Barkley ranch. Her sons, Heath, Nick, and Jarrod, and daughter Audra (who functioned mainly as a love interest) were dedicated to the success of the Barkley dynasty. In numerous episodes it was Mrs. Barkley who rescued her adult offspring from outlaws—even her macho and quite capable cowboy sons.

Mrs. Barkley was a new incarnation of western womanhood. Although she was no Wild West show performer, she held her own in a TV arena dominated by cowboys. On *Bonanza,* for example, there were no female characters at all—let alone a powerhouse like Victoria Barkley. She was the Lorne Greene of the San Joaquin Valley. Stunning in jet-black leather and silver hair, she was a vision of female power. Mrs. Barkley stood in sharp contrast to someone like Miss Kitty on *Gunsmoke,* who wore a sexy satin green dress with black lace and was rarely shown outside of the saloon where she was the queen of nothing and no one but the other bar maids.

It wasn't until I moved to Oklahoma twenty years later that I realized how little I really knew about the women who had inhabited my imagination as a child. When the American cowgirl began to emerge in popular culture through t-shirts, magnets, and in picture books featuring rodeo women, it was clear that cowgirls had a history that had earlier been ignored even as the emblematic Marlboro man reigned supreme. Imagine my delight when I discover the Cowgirl Hall of Fame in Fort Worth, Texas—a magnificent gallery of revisionist history showcasing this new American icon. There are fringed leather costumes belonging to Wild West show performers and television cowgirls, rodeo-prize silver charm bracelets with horses, hats, boots, turquoise hearts, and an array of Western charms, shining rodeo trophy cups, and other artifacts of cowgirl history. There is even an exhibit of the Justin Boots company, a household name in western footwear. The museum boasts a collection of cowgirl boots with feminine designs marketed to women at the turn of the century: lovely pink and blue pastel boots with tooled flowers, hearts, angel wings, and other traditionally female symbols on the finest of leather. The great variety and number of boots produced for women during this era alone suggests that cowgirls who insisted on a feminine standard of fashion in western wear made up an important segment of the boot market.

The western apparel industry catered intensely to women in the late nineteenth century because great numbers of women worked family ranches. The skills they honed there were those later celebrated in rodeos and Wild West show arenas. Like Buffalo Bill, Geronimo, and the other larger-than-life figures who became legends because of the roles they had played on the western frontier, early Wild West show cowgirls were expert ranchers. According to Candace Savage, between 1875 and

1900, a quarter of a million women across the western United States ran farms and ranches of their own, and countless others worked alongside their fathers and husbands. Western states were the first to emphasize the legal claims of married women to their own incomes and lands. Divorce laws were less stringent as well, and despite the environmental hardships, the West was in many ways a place where women had more freedom. As early as 1862, land grants in western states were available to any single, widowed, or divorced woman who was the head of her own household, so the promise of free land had a huge allure for many women who sought to make their own fortunes west of the Mississippi. It was in this region that they found liberties that would not be extended to women in the East for some time.

One young woman who moved west to help run a family ranch was an Oklahoma cowgirl named Lucille Mulhall. Lucille moved to the state as a child in 1889 and lived there most of her life. Her career as a champion roper began when she was barely a teenager. When the mayor of Guthrie, then the capital of Oklahoma, requested that Mulhall children, who were hearty bull riders and steer ropers, entertain visitors, Lucille's father, Zack Mulhall, got the idea to produce his own Wild West show. Mulhall's "roundups," as they were known, included a constellation of performers such as the young Will Rogers, who was billed as the "Mexican Rope Artist." The featured act was Lucille, along with her horse Governor. Hired by the famous Miller brothers when she was nineteen, Mulhall became a renowned member of their 101 Ranch Wild West Show near Ponca City in north-central Oklahoma. She was a cowgirl in the tradition of Annie Oakley, and she performed all over the country, including at Madison Square Garden in 1905.

Michael Wallis explains in his rich history of the 101 Ranch that when Theodore Roosevelt came to Oklahoma City for a Rough Riders reunion, he befriended Lucille's father and watched Lucille perform her rope tricks. A few days after seeing her in the show, Roosevelt went riding at the Mulhall ranch.

It is said that he saw a large grey wolf and commented that he would like to have his hide. According to legend, Lucille ran the wolf down, roped it, killed it, and had the wolf skin sent to Roosevelt. After he became vice president, Roosevelt invited the entire Mulhall family to President McKinley's 1901 inauguration parade. When they visited the vice president's residence, Lucille was very happy to see the wolf's pelt on display in Roosevelt's home!

Although she was twice married and gave birth to a son, Lucille Mulhall was not the kind of woman who could settle down and raise a family. She remained faithful only to her Wild West career and became the first woman in history to produce her own western show. Though she tried many times to retire, she continued to perform, even in vaudeville, until she was middle-aged. When she wasn't on the road with her show, Mulhall spent time at the family ranch in Oklahoma. Unfortunately, Mulhall's life came to an early end—not because she was thrown from a horse, but because she was killed in a car accident. Yet as one of the few featured women of the 101 Wild West Show, Mulhall's legacy in the cowgirl history books remains secure. With speed and grace, this cowgirl roped horses and wrestled steer and then raised her arms in an angelic gesture that showed just how feminine rodeo could be.

Eventually, however, the days of the Wild West shows waned, and competitive rodeo dominated. Bull riding, team roping, and bronco bucking became events linked primarily to cowboys, *not* cowgirls. Barrel racing is the only contest considered by rodeo aficionados to be a women's competition. Shooting out of the gate to run a cloverleaf pattern through barrels at the fastest speed possible is the name of this game, and there are some women and girls who have earned a living by doing just this. They are part of Mulhall's legacy.

Just before attending the International Finals Rodeo (IFR) in Oklahoma City, I meet three women with a terrific commitment to barrel racing. Though they are of different ages and from different parts of the state, they share a common passion for the sport, and it is their passion I want to understand.

One of the younger competitors at the IFR is nineteen-year-old Tiffany Teehee, who is half-Cherokee. Now on a rodeo scholarship at Northeastern State University in Tahlequah, Tiffany will turn pro in another year or so. Her father tells how she has been riding horses since she was five years old, learning to run barrels through a 4H program. Her shiny black hair falls over the coveted IFR leather jacket given to top contenders. I learn through Tiffany that as children, competitors run barrels in pee-wee rodeos and are eligible at first to win silver belt buckles. "I have about three hundred belt buckles," she says with a sly smile. "Then you might win saddles. Or a horse trailer. You don't always win money runnin' barrels." It seems pretty clear that rodeo competitors don't take home a lot of money until they hit the bigger leagues. So what keeps them in the game?

Two other Oklahoma cowgirls, Sallye Williams and Dona Kay Rule, are in a position to explain. They have been barrel racing for over forty years, traveling the hard miles to competitions in Odessa, Texas, or Gilbert, Arizona, or other far-off places nearly every weekend of their lives. Sallye explains rodeo culture to me as we lunch at Cattlemen's Steak House in the Oklahoma City Stockyards. "It thrills me to win," she says, happily, "but it's more than that. It's a lifestyle. I love rodeo people. We spend our lives taking care of animals, working them, and competing with them. And that's what we know. That's almost *all* we know."

Dona Kay Rule says she has never known anything *but* rodeo life. Her father was a team roper, and she began to compete as a youngster. I ask her what it feels like to be a *real* cowgirl in a nation where genuine rodeo cowgirls are in the minority; Dona Kay looks at me and smiles. "Oh," she jokes, "What it *feels* like to be a real cowgirl is that sometimes my elbow aches, other days my back aches. Some days my knee throbs." Dona Kay has been pancaked and kicked in the mouth by horses and has lived to tell about it. "This is a sport that gets in women's blood," she tells me, "and we are always involved with it—training our children or other people's children. The day I graduated from high school I packed my truck and horse trailer and left town with my horse named Cash. I headed for a rodeo in Sweetwater, Texas, and began to earn my living as a pro." She continued to work on ranches as well until she met her husband, John Rule. Together they became co-owners of one of the oldest saddle shops in the country, located in the Oklahoma City Stockyards.

A few nights later, all of us except Tiffany are at the Oklahoma State Fairgrounds Arena, where the fourth and final evening of the IFR competition is under way. Tiffany's father calls to tell me that she has been rushed to the hospital for an emergency appendectomy. This is disappointing because she was third in the standings but will not have the chance to compete. That leaves fourteen other cowgirls ranging in age from twelve to fifty. They are the top contenders in the rodeo circuit.

When barrel racing begins, I stand near the "alley," as it is called, and watch the contestants as they wait for the signal to rush out and around the barrels. Finally, it is Sallye's turn. She looks terrific; her long blond hair flies out behind her as she takes the course. Sallye moves fast and does not touch any of the barrels, and her strong performance puts her in third place. You cannot tell that thirty-eight years separate her and the twelve-year-old girl who takes the buckle that night. Young Mesa Leavitt is simply a blur on the course. She is the top racer in the country, and it shows.

I head out of the arena into the lobby where the atmosphere has been transformed into western Americana: men and women in black cowboy hats peruse the tables of turquoise jewelry, leather belts, horse bridles and saddles, as well as boots, shirts, and other rodeo-a-rama merchandise. Entire families dressed *rancho deluxe* wander around, eating Indian tacos and corn dogs. Although it is a fairly white event, there are a number of African American cowboys in the competition and quite a few African American spectators. The people are all polite:

a man bumps into me because it is so crowded and my Diet Coke spills. "Excuse me ma'am," he says regretfully. "Let me buy you another one." I assure him it is okay, and I walk back into the arena where the bull riding has almost finished. Flags are raised, prizes awarded, and the International Finals Rodeo calls it a night.

While big events like the IFR are thrilling, I am partial to small-town Oklahoma rodeos. They are grand in their own way because they have the drama of the rural setting and are usually held against an outdoor backdrop that is more compelling than an indoor State Fair arena. A few months after attending the IFR, I want to see some local twenty-first-century cowgirls in action, so I go with my family to a tiny rodeo in Blanchard.

As we enter the gate, I realize that I am clearly in violation of rodeo rules of fashion. Every female on the premises, whether she is a participant or a spectator, walks the dusty grounds in Wrangler jeans and boots, western shirt or t-shirt, and cowgirl-hat—with long blond hair (natural or bleached) trailing down her back. Even as a transplanted midwesterner fairly new to these parts, I know better than to stand out like a damn Yankee in a pixie haircut, sundress, and sandals. But it is hot! The 100-degree temperatures have gone to my head, and the result is a fashion faux pas. These girls look so *go west young woman* in all of their rodeo glory. I would have preferred to sweat the evening away in leather boots and Wranglers.

The scent of barbecue wafts from a concession stand across the field, and as the lights come on, there is a sunset in the works behind the stands, the clouds strung in a lavender-and-orange striped affair. An artificial bull is set up near a cinderblock snack bar, and I see a girl who looks to be about eight, a virtuoso rope star of the future wearing an oversized cowboy hat, trying to lasso the leather bull head attached to a box.

In the arena, participants engage in the customary pre-rodeo parade. There are ten men riding the circle, kicking the red dirt up. *But where are the cowgirls?* Suddenly a woman in a lilac western shirt rides past me, and I think she waves and calls my name. When she comes around again, I see that it is none other than my dental hygienist! I never figured her for a cowgirl! It turns out that she is a life-long horsewoman, and will make a good show in the barrel racing event later that evening.

The crowd is asked to stand. Two men in red silk western shirts with the words *Cowboys for Christ* on their backs gallop out into the arena. They carry the flags of both Oklahoma and the United States. The announcer offers a brief prayer and then we all sing the "The Star-Spangled Banner." It grows dark and the flags whip dramatically in the Oklahoma wind. Children hang on to the fence, sucking grape popsicles or waving blinking trinket wands purchased from a vendor. Behind the bleachers, a sea of pickup trucks gleams in the moonlight. While we wait for the first event, Three Dog Night belts from the loudspeaker: "Well I never been to heaven, but I been to Oklahoma . . ." People cheer when they hear the lyrics, and we stand together in a moment of regional camaraderie.

A determined nine-year-old gallops into the ring as barrel racing begins. She makes an impressive turn around the red, white, and blue clover of an obstacle course. Her hat drops behind her back, held just so by a braided cord in a display of rodeo bravado. Perhaps she is an Annie Oakley or Lucille Mulhall in the making, easing in and out of the barrels with a one-with-her-horse elegance. It is tough to admit that I myself will never be more than a wannabe. A collection of boots and tooled leather purses do not a cowgirl make! Still, I am in good company on this night. There are countless others out there for whom the name fits. I whistle loudly, and put my hands together to clap for the girl in suede chaps exiting the arena.

Catherine Hobbs, birdwatcher

The Bird Watcher

∿

My colleague Catherine possesses a sharp wit and a lilting Oklahoma accent. She is a woman who can disagree with a man in a voice so laced with honey that it takes him a moment to realize he has been given what for. She achieves this effect in countless faculty meetings, a skill I admire but can never pull off myself because I am unschooled in the ways of Oklahoma womanhood. Catherine and I have a sisterly bond because we were raised in the same Southern Baptist tradition; we share a familiarity with pulpit-pounding preachers and evangelistic creed. But the similarities end there.

I am an overzealous assistant professor just out of graduate school. Catherine recently earned tenure at the University of Oklahoma and she is hell-bent on dating and dancing for a while. She has little time for me, the nagging kid sister calling for advice. I am a phone person. Catherine can bear no conversation longer than five minutes. "The phone is an instrument for making plans, not gossip," she tells me one day in her sternest sugared tone. I do not give up easily because I trust Catherine to give me the lay of the land and other secrets that will help me survive academe.

When I suggest lunch or the occasional film, Catherine invites me to walk with her at a local pond where kingbirds swoop and cardinals perch in plain view. As the new girl in town, desperate for companionship, I acquiesce. I want to talk shop; Catherine wants to talk snowy egrets and night herons. "What do you think of the work of so-and-so?" I might ask, panting beside her as we circle the pond. Catherine is a very brisk walker. "Oh look, it's a prairie warbler," she says in a voice of soft surprise. It doesn't take me long to learn that if I am going to converse with Catherine, I am going to have to learn a thing or two about birds.

I couldn't care less about any creature sporting feathers. These animals mess on my lawn chairs and the hood of my car. They screech at my cat. Perhaps the reason I think all things avian are loathsome and sinister is that I watched Alfred Hitchcock's *The Birds* too often as a kid. The birds in the film are the physical embodiment of disturbing, shattering forces that threaten all of humanity. They scratch children. They peck people's eyes out. As a result of this movie, I see the Audubon Society as a creepy little organization. Beneath the cheerful exterior of mostly geriatric members with their white tennis shoes and expensive binoculars, something isn't right.

And maybe something isn't right about feigning bird intrigue for Catherine; it's like faking interest in football for a man I hope to date. Lonely as I am for friendship, though, she is worth the effort. I relate to Catherine's birding passion in terms of my own love for junking. Just as I am a scavenger in search of the next old basket or lamp, Catherine is in search of birds both exotic and ordinary—the painted bunting, the yellow-billed cuckoo, the rose-breasted grosbeak.

At the local pond where we walk, the sparrows squeak like unoiled wheels. The sounds are disturbing and I fear birds might defecate on us, but Catherine is unconcerned. She has a CD at home with various birdcalls, and she studies songs of assorted species as though there will be a quiz. At the pond, even invisible birds are noted by my friend as she cocks her head, tuning in to a whistled cadence. "Oh, there's a red-winged blackbird," she exclaims softly. "And a blue jay. No—I'm mistaken. It's a mockingbird in his blue jay mode." Catherine is a regular bird detective.

We plan to meet again at our usual pond one day when the sun is high and the heat excruciating. Catherine is late: I am unhappy when people do not keep their promises to the clock. At last she comes bobbing down the sidewalk, her blunt-cut hair swishing politely. "I'm sorry I'm late," she winks at me. "I was listening to my time-management tape."

I frown, unamused. "It's too hot to walk."

"Not if you put on your heat shield."

"What?"

"Your heat shield. It's a way of setting your mind against the temperatures. Just tell yourself that you have a heat shield of ice on your head, and you won't feel the sun beating down. You can reduce your sense of the temperature by a good four degrees."

I don't want to talk about heat shields or time management, so I just start walking quickly, forcing Catherine to keep up with me. Suddenly, a pearl-gray bird with a pink chest dives beyond us. Its long tail forms a *V*, larger than the rest of its body. The bird moves like a midget helicopter—diving, then moving upward again. "What is that!" I ask, startled and amazed.

"Don't you even know your state bird?" Catherine answers with ornithographic superiority. "That's a scissor-tailed flycatcher."

This little guy is less like a bird and more like a gyroscope. I love his stunning colors and horizontal movements. I quickly mask my enthusiasm because Catherine has been waiting for a moment like this to exert more intense birding influence.

"I've been thinking. You should put up a little feeder in your backyard. Or a birdbath. The poor things are desperate for water. You could at least put out a pot or a bowl so they could get a drink."

"And turn my backyard into a trailer park?" The thought of a stainless-steel pasta bowl on my grass brings to mind a leaking house with containers placed forlornly around to catch rain. I will scout Catherine's birds, but I will not feed or water them.

∽

Some weeks later in a university office, I encounter a painting of the scissor-tailed flycatcher, his majestic back-tail feathers in that familiar long, elegant V. I notice prints of other Oklahoma birds hanging in banks and physicians' offices all over town. They have an eerie presence. I learn they have been painted by the late George Miksch Sutton. Prairie birders think of him as their personal Audubon, a local treasure. A former University of Oklahoma professor and author of a gazillion bird books, Sutton created portraits of feathered creatures that turn up in so many places around town it is downright unsettling. It is a little creepy to meet Oklahoma birds on the walls where I work and do business. I visit the dentist and a great horned owl squints knowingly at me. I go to the bank to sign for a car loan, and a blue jay arches in a menacing pose. At a friend's law office, a boat-tailed grackle stares back with its beady black eyes. George Miksch Sutton is all about town, haunting Norman from his grave with the intensity of Alfred Hitchcock.

Even so, one day I give in and buy a cheap feeder and fill it with sunflower seeds. Red finches, blue jays, and hearty robins appear and soften my heart toward the whole birding enterprise. Their elegance, their delight in feeding makes me realize I have never observed birds before. A pair of Carolina wrens builds a nest in an ornamental birdhouse on my patio, and Catherine comes to watch the mother and father work tirelessly to feed the four beaky babies with fleshy pink limbs. They open their mouths and squeak upon our approach. Only a hard-hearted person could fail to appreciate this sweet wonder.

Catherine and I drink iced tea on my back porch and observe the industrious parents flying back and forth to their brood with insects and seed.

"Carolina wrens are just my favorite bird," she sighs.

"Every bird is your favorite bird."

"Are you sure you wouldn't like to borrow my birdcall CD so that you could learn birdcalls?"

"No thanks. Just because I put up a feeder and am the arbitrary host for a nest of wrens doesn't mean I want to be a bird scholar."

The truth is that I could use a little bird knowledge in order to address the crisis developing in my backyard. An awful smell emanates from the nest, and I call Catherine to say that I think one of the babies is dead.

"You need to get it out of there," she says. "Get some tweezers and pull the dead one out."

"The only tweezers I have are from Beauty Supply and they cost fourteen dollars. I am not getting anywhere near a bird with them. Besides, if I touch the birds, the mother will never come back."

"That's an old wives' tale. Take a little spoon and scoop him from the nest."

I check the Internet, and sure enough, it says that nestlings touched by humans will not deter the mother from returning. I find a plastic spoon and head outside. The other birds cry out as I lift the limp and gooey dead thing from the nest. I toss its tiny remains into my garden and throw the plastic spoon away. Within minutes, the mother is back on the job, feeding her brood.

Each day I watch the baby birds as they develop their little wings and become stronger. It is important to me not to miss the moment they leave the nest, and so I begin to inspect them compulsively, at least twenty times daily.

"Give them some space," Catherine instructs. "They aren't due to fly away for at least another two weeks."

When I cannot stand it, I take one of the babies from the nest and put him on the ground to see if he will try to fly. I realize that no sensitive birder would do this, but my curiosity gets the best of me. The baby wren hops all around, clearly distressed.

The mother and father squeak from the nearby tree as if I am a bird predator, which I am. I go to put the little guy back in the nest, but by this time the other two have squeezed out to see what is going on. They have landed on the potted plants below and are hopping around, greatly disturbed by this bird circus. No one is flying, but no one is in the nest. I call Catherine.

"You did what! Oh, the poor dears . . ."

When I look around again, I see that the entire family is perched in different parts of the tree. In an hour they will be gone, good riddance to me.

Despite my birding faux pas, Catherine suggests that we travel to France together for a conference on global literacy. She pitches the trip in terms of her passion, not in terms of our common research interests. "Imagine," she says with an enthusiasm she must know will be met with skepticism, "We can see French birds!"

"People don't go to France to see birds," I reply, beginning already to consider other possibilities. "They go for the Eiffel Tower and Monet's water lilies." Who would look for birds when they could search for nineteenth-century junk in the Paris Flea Market? I am compelled to call her a birdbrain, but then I fear she might retract the invitation.

As we prepare for our trip, I leave room in my suitcase for the treasures I hope to find at the Marché aux Puces de St-Ouen. Catherine packs two heavy volumes titled *Les Oiseaux du France I and II*. These weighty texts are filled with color photographs of birds named *peregrine, lesser kestrel, redshank, avocet*—and other French-sounding birds that I am willing to bet will not be plentiful in an urban setting.

One August morning we arrive in Paris. Because it is too early to check into our room, we leave our suitcases with the hotel clerk and head to the charming Luxembourg Gardens a few blocks away. The area is filled with lovers, students, and outdoor chess players. We stroll through the famous park past ancient statues, refreshing fountains, and fragrant lavender. Men play boules, and children turn round and round on the antique carousel; there are no exotic birds however—only pigeons that resemble the New York variety, orioles, and a few ducks.

At an outdoor café, French flutters in the background. We sit down and order steaming cappuccinos. I take out my journal to record a few of the events of our journey and Catherine takes out a bird book with postcard-sized photos of *les oisseux francaise*. One sip of my coffee and I am having a perfect French moment. Then the German man at the next table initiates a conversation in English with Catherine.

"Where are you from?" he asks, after he has gleaned her accent—always a giveaway. He pulls his big black-framed glasses from his distinguished face.

Catherine smiles demurely.

"Oklahoma," she adds, before turning back to a picture of a bird that, I am certain, has never ventured near the Luxembourg Gardens.

"Home of the Cowboys and the Indians," the German nods. "The Wild, Wild West!"

We are used to this reception in the United States. Too many people continue to think of the Oklahoma plains as the last holdout for men on horses and American Indians in tipis.

I roll my eyes at Catherine, but it is too late. She has already engaged the gentleman as she has other men in libraries, on buses, and in restaurants. Catherine can emerge from the most unexpected places with a date for lunch. One day as we pushed our trays through a cafeteria line back home, Catherine began talking comets with a man from the meteorology department. They conversed their way past the desserts and the beverages, and as I waited for my change from the cashier I heard Catherine say to the man, "See you Tuesday at twelve." She waved happily, then picked up her tray.

"We're having lunch next week."

"You made a date in a cafeteria line?"

"Well, he knows just about everything about comets!"

The German man leans forward attentively in his chair, and Catherine's routine has begun. I want to write in my journal and keep my perfect moment going, but it is too late. To this European, my friend is the quintessential southern belle, a rare bird perched in the Luxembourg Gardens.

"What brings you to Paris?" he asks, sipping his wine.

"Global literacy," Catherine says, extending her hand. The German reveals that his name is Hans, and, like us, he is an academic, attending a chemistry conference. Catherine and Hans go on for some time in superficial academic banter about the rhetoric of science and semiotics.

I am anxious to check into our hotel room a few blocks away so that I can change my clothes and take a bath. The man wants to know where we are staying, but Catherine pretends to get the name wrong: "Hotel Saint Beatrice," she says, but it is Hotel Le Sainte Beuve. I am grateful she tosses him off her trail.

The lobby of Hotel Le Sainte Beuve is all maroon toile drapes and fuchsia orchids. Lavender fish drift inside a wall aquarium, as if on TV. The clerk hands us a real key, not the plastic card you get in the United States. We drag our suitcases up the winding, black wrought-iron staircase. Catherine fumbles with the lock and voilà! What a sight! The tiny room is covered with yellow wallpaper on which delicate Parisian birds of excellent plumage perch all around. Some are blue, some rust with white markings. My friend laughs with delight. The rest of our chamber is so small that one can hardly move through it to reach the antique armoire and twin beds. Despite these cramped quarters, the room expands a bit with the birds against the yellow heavens.

My first French hotel room ever does not disappoint. There is a tiny balcony from which Paris can be seen in all its glory. The Eiffel Tower rises in the distance in a way I have only witnessed in coffee commercials. I have the inclination to step out on our terrace like Marie Antoinette and cry, "Let them eat cake!" I pause instead to observe that France has nothing on Oklahoma when it comes to the sky, even if everything else here seems to triumph, particularly the cake.

We take out the superb fruit pastries that we purchased before arriving at the hotel and recline happily on our beds. "Tweet, tweet," I say to Catherine, "you got some birdies after all." She smiles and pulls out the weighty ornithological texts from her suitcase and proceeds to study them instead of the magnificent city just outside. The elegant wallpaper wrens and delicate orioles perch all around this charming French aviary. I have to admit, these are my kind of birds. They are not menacing or rough. Not one of them will soil the silk bedspreads. And if I listen carefully, I can almost hear them chirp *bonjour* and *bienvenue* against the pale yellow background that encloses our room with all the citrus perfection of a lemon tart.

Bingo packet sellers

Casinoland

~

Drive any direction toward what you think is the middle of nowhere and you are sure to encounter American Indian casinos rising in all their peculiar glory. I have been told that tribal revenues injected into the communities by casinos are substantial, offering job opportunities and economic growth to impoverished regions. While this may be true, I find it sad that casinos have altered the stark beauty of the prairie.

Casinos such as Lucky Star, Fire Lake, and Riverwind have been named to promote the glories of good fortune. They are persuasively designated to present linguistically appealing roadside diversions and lure them off the road. Some casinos are big gaudy affairs, with flashing lights, while others have the pedestrian aesthetic of an Elks Clubhouse or Moose Lodge. Whatever the exterior appearance, promotional materials suggest that there is a ubiquitous excitement to be found inside all Great Plains gaming rooms. One billboard urges interested parties to call the Wizard of Odds: 1-800-259-LUCK! Another sign offers up a shiny girl in a beaded dress. With her manicured hands full of money and dice, she proclaims, WHO NEEDS FLOWERS?

In truth, such glamorous girls are rarely spotted inside Great Plains casinos. Most female gamblers I see in various establishments are elderly or middle-aged; tapped out by love or life, they pull the lever, waiting for fortune to arrive. I am not a gaming person. I hope never to set foot in Las Vegas again, no matter how family-friendly they claim to make it. In Vegas, men wear entirely too much gold and too many elderly ladies have cigarettes hanging from their mouths. It's depressing to watch people numbly feeding quarters into slot machines, hoping to enter the jackpot stratosphere when all the cherries line up at last.

One Saturday night, though, I take a liking to bingo. In the name of research, my husband and I drive twenty miles to a rural Absentee Shawnee casino to observe a few gamblers in action. Bingo seems more innocuous to me than other gaming activities, given its association with childhood birthday parties and fund-raisers, and for some reason I find that I look forward to sitting in a folding chair for a few hours with dedicated players.

On our way to the casino, we pass a roadside memorial one sees too often along highways in Oklahoma, a cross with a man's athletic shirt draped over it. The blue garment bears the insignia of the Dallas Cowboys, and the arms of the cross poke sadly through the sleeves. Plastic red carnations mark the spot of the loved one's departure in what was most likely a car accident. Many alcohol-related deaths have occurred on this road, resulting in numerous roadside tributes to the dead.

At last we come to the blinking lights on the otherwise darkened prairie. Life-size ceramic Palomino horses stand frozen before a structure that resembles a very grand steakhouse. A few of the windows have been papered over with play money, the faces of Andrew Jackson and Alexander Hamilton employed to get gamblers salivating like Pavlovian dogs. The front doors of the casino open to a garish spectacle: carnivalesque tunes rise from hundreds of slot machines, the beat syncopated to the lights in a haunting vaudevillian invitation.

The bingo hall, by contrast, is quiet as a library; at least two hundred people sit at tables with their daubers poised over game sheets. The somewhat ethnically diverse players are mostly older women. I purchase a lucky green dauber and a Coke while we look for a place to sit. Cigarette smoke hangs over participants like low weather. "I-5," a woman at the microphone calls with conviction. We take our seats near Veronica, a middle-aged Seminole Indian. She is kind enough to instruct us in Crazy Kites, Double Straights, Six Packs, and Black-Out Bingo. An amputee with long hair that extends to the seat of her wheelchair, Veronica explains softly that we are playing Minis, which involves watching several cards at once. A man comes by with sheets for the next game and we're off and running. "O-62," says the caller into a microphone. I'm not sure what we're playing for, but I feel the excitement. The caller moves fast, but a screen on the wall is lit with the numbers in play. Finally someone calls out a *Bingo!* and disappointed players all around me note in hushed tones how very close they were.

During a brief intermission I ask Veronica if she thinks casinos are a good idea for the tribes. Do they help communities in the long run or hurt them? "Depends on the tribe," Veronica says, taking a sip of Coke from a Styrofoam cup. "Take the Seminoles for instance. They spend so much time fighting, they can't get a powerful casino going. The Potawatomies are already working on a hotel for their new casino. That money goes back to help the tribe in ways that are good. We Seminoles get a $250-dollar clothing allowance for our children. What can you really get for $250 dollars?"

I nod and would say more, but another game begins. "This one is Crazy Kites," Veronica explains. "You can win on a diagonal with a square off the bottom." This is news to me. "N-30," says the announcer and I have it. I daub it green. B-6 is the next call and I have that too. Aside from the cigarette smoke I find that I am having fun, thanks to Veronica. "G-50." I have it! I am close to a Crazy Kite Bingo. I'm still not sure what we're playing for. Sometimes it's a pot of money and other times it's a mug. Maybe an ashtray. What do I need with an ashtray? "I–20," the announcer calls. Veronica looks at my card. "You have a bingo, hon! Call it out! Put your card in the air!"

"Bingo!" I say once, then again, louder. I wave my card above my head. A woman comes over to read the number on my game sheet and then asks another player to verify the win. I am asked to sign a paper as my prize is delivered: a small plastic change purse imprinted with the words *Thunderbird Casino*. While the prize is a letdown, winning itself is a thrill. Suddenly I realize I have forgotten to eat dinner and I will be late to claim my child from the babysitter! Without ingesting drugs or alcohol, I have experienced a bingo-induced time-and-space blackout!

That you forget time while you *pay to play* is a principle casinos take to the bank. Gaming houses run numerous promotional schemes to get people in the door and keep them there. Each Wednesday morning, Riverwind Casino hosts a free Senior Citizens' Breakfast that attracts about a thousand older and elderly people for all the eggs and waffles they can eat and ten dollars' worth of free gambling. On the morning I arrive to talk with a few folks, they are lined out the front door of the casino into the parking lot, and there is no shortage of buses from retirement centers dropping them off. Some are in walkers or wheelchairs. Some have oxygen tanks. Despite the overwhelming smokiness of the casino, they have come out in droves for this weekly promotion. Many of them know casino giveaways are an effort to trap them. "You're bound to pay for your breakfast," a woman in a black cowboy hat tells me, "though they tell you it's free. In the end, I pay for my meal three times over."

I take a seat near an elderly couple decked out in gold jewelry and blue gingham western shirts. They humbly bow their heads to pray over their free breakfast in the midst of casino madness. When I ask them if they come often, they nod and smile. They haven't won big yet, but like many people in the room, they have a story of someone who has. A lady with puffy jet-black hair explains, "Last week a friend of ours stood playing the slots. She

Joyce Page, slot machine player

won $2,000 dollars. While she was talkin' to us she won $2,000 again! *Within minutes!*" Stories like this are traded by the casino faithful like baseball cards or church testimonies.

Monday night is Ladies' Nite at Riverwind. Each week, women of all ages are given similar incentives to gamble the night away. From the parking lot it is evident that at least a hundred females are lined out the door to receive ten dollars of free gambling. So many different kinds of women under one roof! Heavy-set women, skinny women, pregnant women, tattooed women, women with dainty gold crosses around their necks. Asian, African American, and Indian women. Women with stiff white hair and girls in their twenties with purple punk hair. Women in nursing uniforms. Elderly women in their Sunday best who walk around the casino clutching their pocketbooks.

One-tenth of the crowd is male, and they look bewildered to be so outnumbered. While the background soundtrack is "Gimme Some Lovin'!" by the Spencer Davis Group, no one would mistake this situation for a pick-up joint. Few men and women are engaged in conversation or even appear to be together; instead, they partner with slot machines in a gaze that is anything but romantic.

A middle-aged woman named Gayle in a *Some Girls are Born Lucky* t-shirt tells me that a few weeks ago she won—and then lost—$5,000 on a slot called Royal Reels. Royal Reels is a popular game that capitalizes on a fashion style appealing to royal wannabees: pink purses with glittery crowns or shirts that read I'M A PRINCESS or IF THE TIARA FITS, WEAR IT! Given this trend, it is easy to see why the two hundred or so Royal Reels machines are well occupied on Ladies' Nite. Gayle hits the play button, while the regal symbols of happily-ever-after (a prince, a princess, a throne, a glass of champagne) blur past. She jokes that she was so broke on the night she won and lost $5000 that she ran out of gas on the way home from the casino and had to call *not* Prince Charming, but relatives—thirty miles away—to rescue her.

For some, gambling is a way to pass the time; for others it is an extreme and doomed form of "entertainment." What is it like to be a person who feels alive only when held in suspense by the possibility of cashing in big? I think of the wrecked men and women I saw years ago in Atlantic City, sobbing with misery and humiliation as they walked the grim, filthy Boardwalk behind the casinos, wringing their hands and crying, "I've lost everything!"

The Oklahoma Association for Gambling Addiction Awareness estimates there are between 35,000 and 105,000 people in the state who currently could be diagnosed as pathological gamblers. At a local Gamblers Anonymous meeting, members bear witness to the devastating consequences of casino compulsion. They tell of friends or family who live out of their cars in casino parking lots, people who surrender completely to the betting life. A woman I'll call Sasha tells the group that she remained glued to her slot machine, even when her friend called to tell her that her gaming center stood in the path of a powerful approaching tornado. "I kept plugging the slot like a zombie with snake eyes," she said. "I just didn't care."

"It's not about the money," adds a woman in a hospital uniform. "Winning $10,000 is like being given a huge stash of crack to smoke. You gamble it 'til it's gone."

Each person in the meeting offers up his or her challenge of the week and expresses gratitude for the time that has passed since his or her last bet. A tentative relief hangs over the room in this small Oklahoma church: it could all change tomorrow and they know it, given the powerful nature of the obsession. "There are over eighty casinos in Oklahoma with thousands of people gambling all hours," one woman says. "There are only eight people in this room tonight, which means we have a lot of empty seats."

Despite the darker side of gambling as an addiction, there is the lighter side of gambling as a business in American Indian communities. Anyone who knows how poorly Indians have been treated in Oklahoma and elsewhere could hardly begrudge them the ability to care for members of their tribes through casino-generated profits. Hospitals and schools have been built, scholarships endowed, and programs for the elderly supported purely through casino profits.

The Chickasaw Nation has a reputation for being a particularly good steward of its casino funds. I talk with members of other tribal gaming commission boards and they tell me that the Chickasaws are the model. They have used casino funds to better the lives of their constituents in ways that other tribes have failed to do. To visit Ada, Oklahoma, is to witness the variety of social programs that exist for the Chickasaw community— many of them for women. A wellness center, a daycare center, a daycare center for mildly sick children, a senior citizens' center, and a variety of other social services aid people who were once members of one of the poorest tribes in the nation.

And what about the employment opportunities casinos offer? I am particularly interested in the managerial and other prestigious jobs offered to women. I am told that at least half of the card dealers at Riverwind are female. I am introduced to Jacy, a twenty-eight-year-old blackjack dealer who is part-Chickasaw and part-Choctaw. After receiving free training from the Chickasaw Nation, Jacy has a skill she could take anywhere in the country where blackjack dealers are needed. She is a lovely girl with straight blond-streaked hair and a beautiful smile. When I catch up with her later in the casino, a semicircle of senior citizen cowboys is gathered around her, holding their cards with hope. Jacy's hands move gracefully, pulling Jacks, Queens, and Aces from the machine and dealing them elegantly.

"Gotta win somethin' here," a man with a handlebar moustache says.

Jacy smiles. "I know y'all are due."

She deals the cards, three cards to each man, but none beats the house, and—just like that—Jacy sweeps all their chips away. I have underestimated the math skills it must take to keep the bets straight. On any given night, tens of thousands of dollars must pass through her hands.

One of the old men looks disgusted. "I guess you better put another hundred on my card." He snuffs out his cigarette authoritatively, and someone from the floor takes his Visa card and helps him place the bet.

"Good luck," Jacy says as she deals again, pushing three cards out in front of each man, sweeping them out like little trains.

The truck driver from Lubbock exhales his cigarette smoke toward the ceiling and sighs: "Somethin's gotta give."

Jacy smiles, and looking good as luck itself, tells the men, "I know y'all are due."

I ask Jacy how she deals with the unruly, unhappy gambler after he or she has lost a sizeable sum of money.

"It happens," Jacy readily admits. "There are people who will look you straight in the eye after they lose and say, 'I can't pay the rent now,' or 'my kids will go hungry.' As though it were all my fault. But you've got to let them vent, and if things get tough, someone from the floor will come up and investigate the trouble."

In the end, it is tough to say what I think about Oklahoma casinos, but I have certainly met some interesting women who work and play at these establishments. And though I do not particularly like games myself, I *am* a risk-taker, and I know what it is to bet on people or lifestyles that will make one broke as any slot machine addict. For this reason I have compassion for the women I see in gaming houses—so much so that I cannot judge the casinos as I once did when I first saw them looming on the horizon.

A few nights after my visit to Jacy's blackjack table, I dream about cards. A crowd gathers round to watch me play. Jacy deals the cards in what looks to be a solitaire game, but I am unsure of the rules. I turn the cards over one by one, but there are no Kings or Queens or Aces or Jacks. Instead, each card holds the face of someone I have met in the tribal casinos. On one card is Sasha from the Gamblers Anonymous meeting, plugging the slots during a tornado. On another card is Gayle, who won and lost $5,000 dollars in one night on Royal Reels and had no gas money for the ride home.

"I need to win, Jacy," I say, but what I really mean is that I need to understand how the riddle of casinos might be solved.

"I know y'all are due," Jacy responds as she taps her lacquered pink fingernails on the soft bright-green surface of the table. I turn over another card, and there is Veronica, who yells "Bingo!" None of it makes sense.

Someone from the crowd taunts me. "Keep playing!" But why? If I stand there long enough, I might understand what it all means. I might figure it out.

At last I turn each card back down and the crowd mumbles its disappointment as I walk away from Jacy and the table, away from the carnivalesque music of the slots and the clouds of cigarette smoke stinging my eyes. Across the large room I keep walking, past people who push buttons of machines that may or may not deliver. I open the front door of the casino and head outside into the parking lot filled with pickup trucks, where slowly and gratefully, I take a deep breath of the April air.

Viola Grounds, Pioneer Queen, and her son

Queens of the Pioneer Outback

 ⁓

There are rooms of curiosities in the No Man's Land Museum worth the distance you must travel across the Oklahoma Panhandle to see them. Consider the stuffed, two-headed calf that lived for two brief weeks in 1932; cases of chiseled arrowheads found in the locality; a peace pipe presented in 1923 to a nearby resident by Blackfoot chief Two Guns White Calf (whose profile graces the "Buffalo Nickel"); and the first printing press to cross the Mississippi!

My favorite exhibit in the museum is a gallery of pictures—some sixty-eight elderly Pioneer Days Queens. Sturdy Ada Quinn, solemn Gwenfred Lackey, smiling Tennie Luther, and stout Lula Wood are a few of the women whose eyes and expressions greet me, their names dating and regionalizing them. Some smile and others face the camera with grim determinism. Each woman lived on the high plains for at least fifty years, and each was a descendent of settlers who laid claim to land when the Panhandle opened under the Organic Act of 1890.

In 1940, Della Keating became the first queen to embody the spirit of the women who "lived on faith and hope and charity

81

alone," according to the Pioneer Days Queen's Creed. Since then, a woman has been selected each year to reign as queen over the Guymon Pioneer Days Festival and Parade.

This year's queen is Viola Grounds, who waves from a black 1956 Buick convertible chauffeured by her son, Sonny, who sports a white cowboy hat and a black leather jacket. Mrs. Grounds is a distinguished-looking elderly woman with short blond hair. Wearing an antique cameo on a black velvet ribbon around her neck, she leads a long parade of Kiwanis and Lions Club floats, tractor drivers, members of 4-H groups, rodeo participants on horses, and clowns who throw candy to children.

I wonder how women like Viola Grounds have made their entire lives in this barren area. The Oklahoma Panhandle is a kind of Yukon Territory, desolate as the moon. Fewer people live here now than in the early part of the twentieth century, when homesteaders succeeded briefly at farming the prairie for wheat until the earth said *no more*. The land rebelled with ten years of dust storms that denied all the plains' earlier promise. From that era come tales of loss and incalculable ruin. Tens of thousands of lives deteriorated in the 1930s in a prairie squalor unrecognized in its magnitude until New Deal photographers captured the devastation and the destruction of a decade's drought and blowing dirt.

A photograph freezes the calamity of a moment, but it obscures the time it took to deliver catastrophe. It silences the voices of people who would tell you how their crops, houses, children, and dignity disappeared over years of days that were supposed to get better but never did. Accounts of this prolonged environmental disaster make one grateful for the ability to draw a clean breath or take in any shade of green on the horizon.

How wonderful to have a house that keeps out the dust and weather, to have plaster walls instead of sod walls where centipedes or spiders roam. What a blessing to have children who are not sick from dust pneumonia and poor nutrition brought on by agricultural ruin.

Timothy Egan explains in his magnificent chronicle of the Dust Bowl, *The Worst Hard Time,* that the Great Plains never recovered from this environmental disaster. President Roosevelt's soil conservation programs helped the plains to stop blowing away, but the region never drew back the population that fled during the 1930s Depression and years of dust storms. Then the Great Plains became an abandoned land in the minds of most Americans.

"The Great Plains," Ian Frazier writes, "are like a sheet Americans screened their dreams on for awhile and then largely forgot about." The tale of western expansion is particularly unromantic if you reflect on the ways in which the spoils of homesteaders came at the expense of the Indians. By the late nineteenth century, lands across Oklahoma (with the exclusion of the Panhandle) were taken from the Indians and opened to settlers in a series of competitive Darwinist land runs.

Consider that only 3,500 people lived across the Panhandle in 1900. By statehood in 1907, more than 35,000 people had moved to the region in an attempt to farm some of the most challenging land in the nation. After a quarter of a century, the dirt was exhausted by poor farming practices, and thousands of pioneers deserted Oklahoma. By 1940, the population of the Panhandle dwindled to nearly 10,000 people, Cimarron County losing nearly half of its pre–Dust Bowl inhabitants.

Today the Panhandle remains a pioneer outback, a rugged and sparsely populated portion of Oklahoma where Dust Bowl survivors and their children lived long before Steinbeck's novel carried the message that anyone with any sense left when the dirt began to blow. People with large families settled upon the prairie with almost nothing to keep them from starving. How they expected to live until they could get a crop was something even they could not explain. All they had to do was to "prove up": prove that they could stay put five years, withstanding heat, isolation, and the agricultural challenges particular to the region—and the land was theirs.

I have a fascination with this territory and the people who have made their homes in a place that broke the hearts of so many. Quite a few individuals remained in the Panhandle despite ecological disasters and drought, among them the Pioneer Queens and their descendants.

What kept these folks from leaving the region for California or some other place where the wind wasn't blowing red dirt and farmers could get a decent rain? These questions bring me to the May Pioneer Days Festival in Guymon to spend a weekend with the people who will grin and shake my hand and say, "Oh, you're from downstate," as if the Panhandle were Alaska and the rest of Oklahoma the lower forty-eight.

Woodward is the gateway to the Panhandle, the last town before the 120 miles of open grassland to Guymon, one-time capital of the Dust Bowl. Many people who live in Woodward consider themselves superior to those in the Panhandle towns up the road. When I tell the cashier at the gas station that I am going to Guymon, he says, "Don't bother." Then he smiles. "There's nothing in that town, and you have to drive through a lot of nothing to get there."

I pay the cashier and observe the small-town standard fare in Woodward: a café named Polly Anna's, a barbershop with a candy-cane stripped pole, a bar called The Lounge (open at 10 A.M.), and a museum that boasts one of the largest collections of ceramic toothpick holders in the world. Like most small towns on the Oklahoma plains, Woodward's religious eccentricities are readily apparent. There is a cinema turned mission church where the phrase LOST JOYFUL NOISE FOUND appears on the marquee. I retain these words like enigmatic fortune-cookie slips I have stuffed in my pocket, intrigued by predictions I'm not sure I understand. The fact is I do find lost joyful noise in the 120 open miles between Woodward and Guymon; that is, if you consider the sounds of silence a kind of noise (à la Simon and Garfunkel). One must drive Panhandle highway OK 412 to

see why this region is called No Man's Land. Only two gas stations exist along the way, and the absence of a generic ensemble of fast food chains and other icons of American business settles my mind. The constant play of sun and shadow on this grassland emphasizes the prairie's lonely immensity.

Spend a day or two in this country, and the whole flat world of grass and sky will remain in your sensory reaches like a boat that continues to rock in your mind long after you've left the water or like a carnival ride that continues to thrill you long after your exit. This prairie gets inside your head, all the bleached light and red dirt against a sky as blue as Mary's holy robe.

I would live on the high plains except I couldn't, hundreds of miles from hospitals, libraries, and yes—I hate to admit it—a decent mall. I don't have what it takes to live in No Man's Land, so I will always be the tourist from downstate, photographing abandoned barns and houses with a stranger's eyes.

Each year a new Pioneer Days Queen is crowned at a luncheon attended by local people as well as former queens. The tradition began almost half a century ago at the Dine-A-Teria in Guymon. The Chamber of Commerce now sponsors the event. After the parade, I head to the Ambassador Inn where 2009 queen Viola Grounds is to be honored. The menu is a plate lunch of chicken-fried steak and all the trimmings at $9 per person. However, when we arrive we are told that "no one need pay, since Viola's son is picking up the tab."

"It is a great honor to be chosen Pioneer Days Queen," Viola tells me when I meet her for the first time at this event. She adds that it has inspired fond memories of past celebrations. For many years of her married life, she and her husband, Ralph, rode horseback together in the Pioneer Days parade. Ralph proudly saddled a horse or drove one of his antique vehicles, carrying each of his grandchildren. Sometime in the early 1950s, Viola won the award for "best-dressed" woman rider.

At the luncheon Viola tells how in the late 1930s she "took up housekeeping" as a young woman "with a broom and a shovel, not a dainty little dust mop." She taped around all the windows and hung wet sheets around her baby's crib to try and keep the dust out. In the mornings, the only white spot in the room would be the pillows where her family's heads had been.

Born in 1918 to German parents, Mary and George Lundgrin, who had immigrated from Russia, Viola is a first-generation American. German was spoken in her home and in the small community of other immigrants where she was raised near Hooker, Oklahoma. Viola knew little English when she began her education. Her older brother, George, drove her one and a half miles to school in a horse and buggy.

In 1936 Viola Lundgrin married Ralph Grounds in a double wedding with her sister Leona and Harry Feil. The reception took place in a barn on their parents' farm. Kerosene stoves and ovens rendered baking hens with dressing. Members of the community came and brought food as well. An old tradition was to snatch the bride's shoes and sell them to the men in the wedding party. Later, Viola found her shoes nailed to a post but jokes that she "never got any money for them."

Ralph worked in the grocery store for $1.25 per day and Viola was employed by the Sears Variety Store for $.75 per day. Later, Viola became a mother, then grandmother. In her spare time she took up oil painting and helped paint backgrounds for local proms and theatre productions.

A slight woman, Viola is delicate in appearance in her navy-blue blazer and high-necked blouse with the antique cameo at her neck. She does not have the rugged look of many of the women whose portraits hang in the No Man's Land Museum. I wonder about the other Pioneer Days Queens before Viola who have passed on. What about those who came during the land runs and lived in sod homes, the true generation of *Little House on the Prairie* women?

Fortunately, a man named Bill Bridges has made it his business to get the history of former queens down on videotape—a practice he began in the 1980s. The women in his videos tell stories of coming west in covered wagons, hard-life tales of their "trials on the trail." Most of the women focus not on the struggles they faced getting to this region of the country but the catastrophes they confronted once they got to a land of little rain and few resources.

Many mention the Great Depression, timed with the decade of storms known as the Dust Bowl or the "Dirty Thirties" as they are often called.

"So many people left in the Dirty Thirties," Mr. Bridges observes. "Why did you stay?"

"It was home," explains Mrs. Essie Hoobler, Pioneer Days Queen 1981. "We didn't know if there would be anything better."

Dovie Huff, 1988's Pioneer Days Queen, adds that "when the dirt was so terrible, a light bulb just wouldn't show in a room."

Other women around the tables nod in agreement.

Some Pioneer Queens have tales that make those from the Dust Bowl pale in comparison. As a five-year-old child, Velma Bingham McClung (Pioneer Days Queen 1985) watched her father and brother die of typhoid fever within days of one another in 1905. She and her twenty-five-year old mother, Leona

Bartley Bingham, were left alone on the homestead. However, Mrs. Bingham refused to give up their claim. Velma recalls:

> *Our dugout had two rooms and two outside doors. One for the front room and one for the kitchen. This was another feature the other dugouts didn't have. Even though it was a wonderful dugout, it still wasn't snake-proof—I think perhaps because we didn't have screens. . . . Our windows were just above the ground. Mama could see out, but I couldn't until I got older. Many times early in the morning we saw a coyote look in our window, but the minute we made a move, he immediately took off. . . . While our dugout was cozy on the inside, it wasn't practical against keeping Mother Nature's elements out. Jack rabbits dug a hole at one side of the dugout unnoticed by mama. It came a terrible rain and the hole made by the rabbits and water covered the floor 6 inches deep.*

Velma's mother routinely slept with a loaded .32 caliber revolver on the chair. "Since our door was handmade, it couldn't be very securely locked. Therefore, she placed a butcher knife between the casing and the door to further ensure our safety."

Despite the hardship, Velma tells of ice-cream socials and cake parties where people drove twenty miles to Guymon to get ice and carry it back wrapped in blankets so it would not melt. There was singing and dancing, and children were later put to sleep lying in all directions on the beds.

At ninety years of age, Velma's articulate manner and good sense of humor make her appear much younger. She recalls how during her childhood her mother was courted by other widowers in the area and how there were numerous presents for Velma under the tree at Christmastime from men who had their sights on Velma's mother. "Grandma Bartley said they just wanted to salt the calf to catch the cow." Eventually, Velma's mother did remarry, and her family moved to Guymon so that she and her stepbrother could go to school.

When Velma herself married and had children of her own, she remained in No Man's Land. She worked in a bank where she did not reveal that she was married because married women were discouraged from working outside the home. She was also a postmistress for a time. Like many of the elderly women at the luncheon, she emphasizes the many blessings of her life and the extraordinary period of history in which she has lived: "If I could have chosen the era that I would have preferred to live, I couldn't have chosen one with as many changes as the past eighty years: cow chips to gas heating, kerosene to electric lighting, horses to space travel, and slates to computers."

Interviews with former Pioneer Queens are interrupted briefly by emcee Jo Scott, who announces that the ladies will recite the Pioneer Queen's Creed and sing "Home on the Range," the official Pioneer Days Queen Song. She asks a room of women aged eighty and older to stand. They struggle to rise from their chairs and then together recite the Creed:

Dear Father, grant that we meet each year in the Pioneer Spirit of Kindness, fellowship and brotherly love. Dedicated to pay homage, to keep in our minds and the minds of others the memories of those mothers who lived on faith and hope and charity alone—who instilled character, moral stature and admirable enthusiasm to their future descendants. Bequeath us, O Lord, the power to achieve the patterns they set before us.

Doris Meyer (Pioneer Days Queen 2002), a bent-backed woman with a very high hairdo, heads to the piano to accompany the women as they sing their official song. Mrs. Meyer pounds out a few chords, and the women begin in shaky soprano unison, "O give me a home, where the buffalo roam, where the deer and the antelope play . . ."

After the singing, Jo notes that a few of the former queens have passed away in the last year. "We will now light a candle in memory of them." Doris Meyer stands to do the honors, but though she is a skillful pianist, she cannot light the candle. Another former queen hobbles over to give it a try, but she, too, fails. Finally a man in a white cowboy hat comes forward and makes sure that the wick catches light. Jo reads the names of the deceased—and a prayer is offered on their behalf.

The No Man's Land Museum provides biographies of every queen, many written by the women themselves. I am especially impressed with those written by Mrs. Lyda V. Beasley Mayer (Pioneer Days Queen 1958), a gifted writer with interesting stories to tell. Here she vividly evokes the power of prairie fires:

> To never have witnessed a prairie fire racing across the prairie, at times equaling the speed of the winds in its mad, merciless, riotous behavior, is to have no inkling of what it really was. Drifting "whither the winds bloweth," it spread like oil upon water; it licked its fiery, flaming tongue in all directions seeking what it could devour. Its distressing roar and crackling in the burning of dry brush made the natives quake in horror, and it left a black and smoldering trail of desolation in its wake.

I am intrigued by Mrs. Mayer's adventures as well as those of all the women, even though some women at the luncheon insist that there is nothing remarkable about their lives or about the place they have lived. I have to disagree. Essie Hoobler (Pioneer Days Queen 1981) made 195 quilts in a ten-year period! Noreen Ester and Emma Folker each gave birth to nine children! Buffalo Bill paid a visit to Anna Calvert (Pioneer Days Queen 1948) and her father in their soddie! These women built a culture and a life in a place where many people failed to do so.

Most of the Pioneer Days Queens at the luncheon have had their say, except for Queen Bessie Zentz (1989), who sits contentedly at a table festooned with little covered wagons and copper cowboy boots. She is at home in her small sorority. Like her sisters, she is outfitted in a pioneer dress with a black-and-white cameo at her neck. All of the queens have spoken but her. Bill Bridges asks if she has any tales to add about her trials on the trail.

Mrs. Zentz smiles sweetly and shakes her head. "I really don't," she says. "I love this country. I've traveled through the years to Europe and Hawaiya . . . and . . ." The elderly lady stops to reflect for a moment as if she is about to say something that will shock the interviewer but certainly not the rest of the room. "And I *still like the Panhandle of Oklahoma!*" she says feebly, but firmly. Mrs. Zentz grins at the other Pioneer Days Queens seated at the table and reaches out to touch one of the little covered-wagon centerpieces with a trembling hand. "I think the best people are here."

Tornado Alley Rollergirls

Roller Dolls

◞

It is the evening of the second annual Turnpike Trauma Roller Derby Tournament at the Farmer's Market in downtown Oklahoma City, where a bout between OKC's Tornado Alley Rollergirls and the women of Tulsa's Green Country has been dubbed "Mayhem at the Market." An eclectic crowd of spectators includes farm families with rowdy children and young women holding hands at the concession stand. Home-baked organic treats are for sale on the sidelines by hippy mothers working for this evening's breast cancer fundraiser. Next to them, event promoters offer reasonably priced t-shirts and bumper stickers with catchy slogans like, I ROCK—THEREFORE I ROLL; ROLLERGIRLS RULE; and MY MOMMY PLAYS ROLLER DERBY! In the bleachers fans stomp and cheer : "RD! OKC! RD! OKC!" What a lively introduction to the twenty-first-century version of the sport! I am about to find out, however, as a coach tells aspiring rollergirls in the film *Whip It*, "There is more to derby than fishnets and picking out a tough name."

But who can deny that black fishnets and tough names are an enticing part of women's roller derby? Our home team, the

93

Tornado Alley Rollergirls, coached by Outlaw Josey Whales and Mel A Dramatic, are in blue and orange. The Green Country Girls sport black and green. They race on old-school quad skates and dress the part of hard-hitting roller derby women. Among the Tornado Alley Rollergirls are Devious Pixie and Lady Gore Gore. Standout players for Green Country are Rosie the Wrecker and Syko Path. Some team members make up their faces with glitter stars and streaks of red war paint, their hair in wild pigtails or wacky braids.

I watched women's roller derby as a kid with my grandfather in southern Ohio in a pre-cable, two-channel zone encompassing Kentucky and West Virginia. On Sunday afternoons we cheered women on in a world where there was more skirmish than skating. The staged catfights, pushing, and hair-pulling gave derby a big-time wrestling feel. In 1972, I was a fifth-grader with metal lock-and-key skates that slipped over my shoes. On the rough asphalt of my neighborhood, I was Derby Diva, skating around the block in a plaid skirt and white kneesocks. I recall seeing Raquel Welch in *Kansas City Bomber* as K.C., the single mom who laces up to earn a living for her two kids. She chewed gum and sped around the circle, pushing even the toughest girls to the rail. Sadly, however, the rowdy, raucous sport I loved rolled into obscurity suddenly, and I was left to wonder what happened to all those women whirling around the track on Sundays. My grandfather (in the days before remote control and cable channels) simply got up one afternoon and turned the channel to professional bowling. My skates began to rust in the garage, never to fit again.

Thirty years later, I notice signs for bouts between the Oklahoma City Victory Dolls and the Tornado Alley Rollergirls in store windows around town. One poster advertising a SHOOT-OUT AT THE OKLAHOMA CITY ROLLER DERBY CORRAL flaunts a tattooed cowgirl sitting on a fence in a short skirt, tube socks, and white roller skates. I have heard about the roller derby resurgence but have yet to witness it in its twenty-first-century incarnation. Unlike the professional derby I watched as a kid, these rollergirl teams are all volunteer. They skate to raise money for animal shelters and (somewhat ironically, given the hard-hitting nature of this sport) victims of domestic violence. Some say that twenty-first-century women's roller derby remains a campy, feline version of pro wrestling. Others argue that the WFTDA (Women's Flat Track Derby Association) sets a standard for genuine athleticism and that it therefore should be a professional sport. While roller derby is undeniably kitschy, players take the game and themselves very seriously. But sport or no sport, athleticism or no athleticism, the carnivalesque nature of women's roller derby may prevent it from ever making it to the cover of a Wheaties box. Then again, who knows?

We are in the "suicide seats," where an out-of-control roller-girl might tumble into our laps at any minute. Carson is ecstatic, munching on a homemade oatmeal cookie and screaming for the Tornado Alley Rollergirls. Frank is happy because the generous concession stand cashier threw in four free meatballs with his order. I study the program and the large number of ads for chiropractors and massage therapists—services roll-ergirls would undoubtedly need. The diverse crowd creates a genuine atmosphere of goodwill in the house. Suddenly, a sexy brunette in an evening gown, announcer Katz Me Ouch, calls us to attention: "Good Evening Ladies and Gentlemen! I want to hear YOU screaming for your girllllzzzz!"

A cowbell clatters as Dirty Dawnie, Calamity Jade, Scarla O'Teara and other team members glide to their positions. I am intrigued by women who are willing to put their bodies on the line for a lot of glory and no pay. What about the knee injuries and the trips to physical therapists? Personally, I am all style and no stamina. While I might enjoy now and then wearing an old cheerleader skirt or a tutu, or a jersey with an intimidating moniker (the look can be described as '50s pin-up model meets the *Rocky Horror Picture Show*), I would have to draw the line at actual participation. My bones ache enough as it is. And I could never adopt the tattoos that appear to be a central feature of the uniform. Rollergirls and tattoos are said to go together like beer and BBQ. It's tough to imagine myself inked with even the most feminine of butterflies, delicate cherry blossoms, or red-winged hearts, let alone some of the body art that I see skating by. A royal-blue and robin-red Wonder Woman on the arm of one girl stands out, as does the green Tinkerbell on the shoulder of another. One woman has two large pink-and-black Hello Kitty tats on the back of each thigh. I cringe when I think about how these tattoos will play out in later life, on aged skin. But in the present moment all this ink gives rollergirls an edgy look—and no one can underestimate how image can ignite strategy at any moment.

Roller derby is a cross between hockey, football, and NASCAR. Hard hits and scary spills are par for the course for derby girls, and track rash and bruises serve as their battle scars. How do you play the game? Five skaters from each team take the floor during any one scoring session: one pivot, one jammer, and three blockers. Pivots and blockers from both teams make up the pack. Pivots control the speed of the pack and jammers score points by continually lapping around them. The jammer gets one point for each opposing player she passes. But weaving through the pack is like trying to run the gauntlet. The jammer is hit and shoved to the side by blockers trying to derail her. The jammer that laps the pack first is considered the lead jammer and can stop the match at any time as a strategic maneuver by placing her hands on her hips. Scoring sessions (called jams) last for one minute. Jams are strung together into quarters; four quarters equal a bout. Bouts last for approximately one hour.

Team participation comes with a price. Teams practice at least three times a week; some say all this activity is like having another full-time job. I am told by rollergirls at Mayhem at the Market that derby is a lifestyle—and they are in it for life, on and off the track. Like other women I have interviewed, ex-rollergirl Stardust Wunch, whose roller name is Scardust, proclaims that derby is *all* about the sisterhood. "Sisterhood is huge," she explains. "We really hang together. A while back we had a teammate whose boyfriend was abusive. She told him to move out and he wouldn't, so one day nine of us showed up, had the locks changed, and put his stuff in the front yard while he was gone. When he came back, he took his clothes, a few items, including the TV, and left." Stardust stops for a minute to take a drag from her cigarette, then exhales. In a take-no-prisoners tone she adds, "What else you gonna do with nine rollergirls on your porch?"

"They'll be talkin' about this tomorrow in church!" Katz Me Ouch taunts over the microphone as a new jam begins. Mistress Doom, for the Green Country Girls, comes around the pack, an expert jammer. She breaks through and scores four points for her team. But as she passes one skater, a block sends a Tornado Alley Rollergirl off the track, and she lies on the floor clutching her arm. While the refs rush to her side, players from both teams go down on one knee in a show of support for their fallen sister. She is helped to her feet and everyone applauds.

The bout continues with the Green Country Girls in the lead. In the audience, fans hold up signs that say I LOVE MY SKATING DIVA and SKATE: DON'T HATE. It's tough to think about the sisterhood when you watch women slamming into other women. To say nothing of the ways in which a skater can play dirty. There are plenty of legal moves for sending an opponent flying into the third row, but throwing elbows, tripping, and clotheslining opponents by linking arms with a teammate can land a rollergirl in the penalty box. Fighting or tripping can get a skater kicked out of the game.

This is not a great night for the Tornado Alley Rollergirls (the Green Country Girls win, 82–52), but I have found some new heroines. I look forward to meeting them over pizza in the near future to learn more about the sport. Carson buys an autographed poster for me with the Tornado Alley Girls' signatures and the three of us head to the car with hundreds of other twenty-first-century derby fans.

When I tell my acupuncturist friend in Seattle about the women's sport I am following, she pooh-poohs its status as any kind of feminist enterprise. "It's all about the sisterhood!" I argue, but she will have none of it. "These women try to kill each other! Then they end up in my office with all kinds of physical problems and no health insurance."

I suggest to my friend that perhaps the women of the Great Plains practice a *kinder, gentler* form of derby; the spectators certainly aren't the beer-chugging, swearing sideliners that appear in a documentary called *The Rise of the Rat City Roller-girls*, where some of the player comments about the thrill of derby aggression are a little frightening. "I like to knock the snot out of people," explains Melicious, a young woman who looks more like a ballerina than a rollergirl. "I get high every time I bump some chick to the ground."

One of her teammates agrees. "There's nothing like knocking women to the floor! It's a real stress reliever!"

I want to see how the Tornado Alley Rollergirls compare to the Rat City Rollergirls or the women in the documentary *Brutal Beauty*, where the love of aggression seems the main impetus for derby. Ten Tornado Alley Rollergirls meet me for pizza in Oklahoma City, and there is an aura of celebrity around the table, though the members of this team don't get paid for their time on skates. Most of them tell me that they took up derby after their divorces, because they wanted to be more social, but they didn't want to go to bars. "The average age for women who play derby is thirty," explains Tori Slaymost, mother of two. Ni-Trick Acid, one of the few African American Tornado Alley girls, is twenty-nine. She tells me about her introduction to the game: one day she was at a skating rink for a kid's birthday party, and rollergirls began to come in to set up their equipment for a bout. "The minute I saw them, I knew I wanted to play."

"But aren't you afraid of getting hurt?" The chicken in me cannot imagine risking my health as a real-life rollergirl, especially considering some of the knee and neck surgeries these players have undergone. "Don't you think about how these injuries might affect you when you are older?"

"That's what nursing homes are for," Rita My Fist responds non-chalantly. We all laugh, but I don't get it. Each woman shows me her battle scars: traces of knee-surgery and neck-surgery incisions; rods in one arm or another.

"You can eliminate most injuries by learning how to fall," explains Mary Jane Mayhem, as though landing know-how offers all the protection and rationale one needs to play. The falls have names like "Rock Star" (falling on both knees—picture a heavy metal star, knees down, playing guitar rifs); "the Superman" (sliding face-down, arms out on the floor). No matter how you fall, you must always close your hand into a fist; otherwise, your fingers may be mangled by someone else's skate.

Case in point: Rollergirl husband and ref Cap'n Ron, who joined us for pizza, pulls up a gruesome picture on his iPhone from a derby website. It is a woman's hand, minus her middle finger. We wince and groan at the gruesome photo but rollergirl Lil Viotch is unphased. "Hey," she says without blinking, "she can still skate."

For all their bravado, the Tornado Alley Rollergirls emphasize that they take no pleasure in hurting another player. "I feel really bad if I hit someone hard," says Mary Jane Mayhem. "Oh yeah," Mel A Dramatic, agrees, slapping her hands to her eyes. "Remember when the ambulance came for Toxic Tequila and all the girls were crying, lined up beside the stretcher? We told her we were going to cancel the bout, and she motioned no! with a profound hand signal. And so we played on."

When I ask the ten girls gathered at the table whether or not they think women's roller derby should become an Olympic sport, they react like suffragettes who've been denied the vote.

"Give me a break!" says Kaysa Payne. "They make trampoline jumping and curling legitimate Olympic competitions and keep derby out? Really? Curling? You tell me how that's a sport!"

The Tornado Alley Rollergirls are adamant that derby will one day take its place at the Olympics, but Mel A Dramatic disagrees. "Roller skating has *never* been taken seriously. Think about it!"

A three-second air of melancholy hangs over the table before someone mentions the baby shower for their coach on Saturday. More than a few players have been sidelined by pregnancy, but then again, a baby is just a derby cheerleader in the making. Malice in Underland sells derby baby clothes on the side: onesies with skulls, and tiny tutus. Some derby children sport these outfits at bouts, including colored wigs and crazy make-up.

I figure that having pizza with the team makes me an elite member of their fan club, and I vow to dress derby at the next bout, in a Tornado Alley Rollergirls sweatshirt at the very least.

When I hear that the Tornado Alley Rollergirls are holding an expo down the street in Norman at StarSkate, our local skating rink, I try to convince Carson to come along. He is reluctant because he is having a perfectly good time building Lego starships and watching SpongeBob. "Come on," I beg, "I'll let you drink Coke."

"Say no more, Mama!" He grabs his coat and heads for the car.

Tornado Alley skater and communications director My Oh Mya greets us as we enter the rink. Decked out in a blue wig and blue-glitter eye shadow as she sells Tornado Alley Girl sweatshirts by the door, Mya has just returned from Nationals in Chicago, and, before that, Roller Con, a derby convention held in Las Vegas each year. I desperately want a sweatshirt, but there is only one left (an extra small), and so I will have to wait for another bout to look like a true fan.

The daughters of rollergirls are decked out on this occasion in pink-and-turquoise tutus (purchased from Malice in Underland). One of them is five-year-old Zoe, who has come with her grandmother to watch the expo. "What do you think of your rollergirl mom?" I ask.

The kindergartner with a long blond ponytail and freckles is shy and refuses to make eye contact. "Cool," she says, looking straight ahead, swinging her legs as she bites into a messy nacho chip, catching a string of melted cheese below her chin just in time.

"What do you like best about the Tornado Alley Rollergirls?" Zoe smiles big. A no-brainer. "I like them because whenever it's someone's birthday, they give the rollergirl a cake and the team dances around her on skates." Who wouldn't like to celebrate one's birthday in this fashion?

On the floor, the girls are skating a scrimmage-style expo, and the atmosphere is all fluorescent lighting and light rap music in the background. Katz Me Ouch is there, in street clothes instead of evening gown, calling the bout from a microphone behind the skate-rental desk. I hardly recognize her aside from her voice: "You better watch out for Rosie's 'crazy eye' tonight!" "No one's gonna escape Dirty's booty!" "Kasa Payne is gonna deliver her usual ouch, so you better watch out girlzzz!"

Tonight, after this expo ends at 10 P.M., the Tornado Alley Rollergirls will be out together while the rollergirl grandmothers or husbands put the kids to bed. They will sing their karaoke theme song, "Don't Stop Believin'" by Journey. They will drink beer and recount their evening of glory. I am envious, as I leave the expo before nine to get my derby boy to bed. We climb into the station wagon (a car no self-respecting rollergirl would drive), and I wish I had some derby courage to take the edge off middle age. Would that I had a menacing rollergirl name or at least a team sweatshirt. But I will be at the OKC Farmer's Market in January, when the next bout begins, following this team loyally through the stormy season that gave the Tornado Alley Rollergirls their name, beholding all the force of their marathon on wheels.

Nhung Le Nguyen, Asian district jeweler

Lady of Jade

～

I head to the Asian district whenever I am irritated by aspects of Oklahoma's regional culture. News anchors with overly twangy accents and redneck road ragers. Business people who shamelessly fuse evangelism and capitalism, placing gaudy crosses on commercial signs as if to say *Trust me, I'm a Christian*. For the most part I truly love where I live, but there are times when I long to escape from a place with so many misspelled billboards. (Once, on a seventeen-mile stretch, I saw HARD BODYS—a gym; WE BYE USED CARS—an auto dealer; and ENGLSH: AMERICA'S OFFICAL LANGUAGE—a political announcement). If there is one thing I can say about Ohio, where I come from, the billboards are usually spelled right.

In moments like these, when I feel a twinge of homesickness, I wander to a part of Oklahoma City some call "Little Saigon." All along Classen Boulevard, pink neon signs advertise Indochinese food, videos, and clothing. Red paper lanterns hang from merchants' ceilings as though each day were New Year's. Though I know it is presumptuous to compare my own

geographic vertigo to that of Asian Americans who came to
the United States under duress, I do take comfort from being
around those who have landed here with me on the eccentric
prairie.

Were it not for the Vietnam War and the ultimate fall of
Saigon in 1975, this lovely district might never have emerged.
Americans who sympathized with victims of the Communist
regime took in thousands of "boat people." Throughout the
1970s, church members in Oklahoma City sponsored refugees
from Southeast Asia, who must have found Oklahoma a strange
new world indeed, a place absent of the deep greens and water
of the Mekong Delta or the mountains of Vietnam's central
highlands. Nevertheless, the area along Classen Boulevard was
born out of the desire of the Vietnamese to make a new home,
and its residents have formed a thriving community, bringing
international flair to cowboy country.

One Saturday morning I wander into a store that becomes
my personal Tiffany's, a Far Eastern treasure chest called My
Ngoc ("Beautiful Jade"). The entrance to My Ngoc is covered by
wrought-iron bars to discourage the criminal element. A hand-
written note on a cardboard sign reads PRESS BUZZER TO ENTER.
I come here to stare at jade for long periods of time when I have
what Holly Golightly calls the "mean reds." I am restored to
peace by apple-green Buddhas and bangles streaked in dark-
emerald jadeite ink, grass-colored Burmese stone carved into
delicate fish, intricate butterflies, and circular pendants bleeding deep Rorschach greens. The Chinese believe that jade pro-
tects one against evil and shields against disaster. I buy a sturdy
jade bangle and it becomes my talisman against displacement, a
meditative gem to ward off melancholy and loss.

A small black dog barks, and through a doorway of trans-
lucent yellow beads, Nhung Le Nguyen emerges. She wears a
simple tailored jacket, black pants, and a beaded jade bracelet
on her wrist. The beads clink on the glass when she puts her arm
on the case and asks, "May I help you?" For years Nhung Le and
I have known each other simply as merchant and customer. She

teaches me that the best jade comes from Burma and how to spot the dyed color and poor clarity of an inferior piece. Moving easily between English and Vietnamese, Nhung Le caters to customers who fan out stacks of hundred-dollar bills for pearls from Japan, white diamonds from Belgium, or the eighteen karat gold chains that shimmer warmly in the cases.

Nhung Le has sent her four grown sons to college through her labors, and much to her dismay, none of them are married. "All this jade," she tells me one day as she gestures toward her jewelry kingdom, "and no daughters-in-law or granddaughters to wear it." Her husband, Gio Nguyen, works in the store, selling watches and greeting customers, but the jewelry trade has been in Nhung Le's family for a long time, and it is her know-how that has made her the Asian district's most successful business woman. For over thirty years, Nhung Le's store has been open seven days a week, from 9:30 A.M. to 6:30 P.M. Though she already has made her fortune and her husband urges her to close at least four days a month, the jewelry empress says no. "What would I do at home?" she asks. "All of the people I want to talk with come here."

A constant stream of customers buzzes at the door, waiting to be let into the house of jade. One woman wants to have a gold bangle she purchased from Nhung Le years ago resized. Another comes with her fiancé to look at wedding rings. A tall man brings a jade necklace for appraisal. Nhung Le breaks into the harsh consonants of Vietnamese; I wait outside that discourse for her to return.

When she turns her attention to me, I ask Nhung Le about a large photograph that hangs on the wall behind the counter: villagers in mushroom-shaped conical hats bicycle past a My Ngoc store marquee that lights a busy street in Quy Nhan. Nhung Le takes down the gold-framed photo like an esteemed gem. "This was my father's business in Vietnam," she says. "When the Communists came, they took everything. They raided My Ngoc and our apartment above and took every pearl and diamond, all the jade we had."

Forced out of a luxurious home, Nhung Le's family fled south to Saigon. Each evening at seven, there was knocking at the door and everyone was called into the street. The able and the disabled, the young and elderly alike, were forced to cheer on Communism, the new government, and "Uncle Ho" Chi Minh. "They tried to rally the people," Nhung Le says, "but if you refused to leave your house, they sent you to a re-education camp. Each night we stood there for hours while they talked nonsense." Nhung Le's husband, a South Vietnamese soldier, was imprisoned in what came to be called the Hanoi Hilton. He would not see Nhung Le or their four children for over eight years.

As the North Vietnamese swept further south, Nhung Le's family lost its status and past lifestyle. According to Nhung Le, there was nothing the grains of Communism did not dust, even elementary education, where the opportunity for curricular propaganda was great: "My children brought home second-grade math problems that read, 'If you have two dead American GIs and you find three more, how many dead American GIs do you have?'"

As a child in the 1970s, I was sheltered from the cultural and political revolution shaking the United States. Growing up in Columbus, Ohio, during this time, I registered that I was part of an era dominated by wide sideburns, big sunglasses, and shag carpeting, but I remained oblivious to the political events of the day. I was unaware that up the road in Kent, college students protesting the Vietnam War had been shot by National Guardsmen. My parents were twenty-something young Republicans with a brick ranch house and two children, their lives securely anchored in the Midwest. While the world shifted to a new logic of disorder, I inhabited a neighborhood on the outskirts of national frenzy where the border between my life and the wider chaos was sealed. Some families may have had Dylan whirling on the record player announcing unapologetically that "the times they are a changin," or Janis Joplin singing of sexual liberation in gravel-voiced shrieks, but my parents' music, at least partially, was the fence that kept the revolution out. Glen Campbell echoed through our house as one of the last enforcers of conventionality, announcing that all was still right in the world.

Even Campbell had one song about Vietnam (written by Oklahoman Jimmy Webb). I listened to the tune about the soldier in Galveston who thinks of a lovely girl when he leaves for Southeast Asia. When my cousin Gil was killed in the war when I was seven, the bubble of my suburban safety burst. I did not know that Galveston was in Texas, or Hanoi was in Vietnam, but I learned that war was serious business as I took in Walter Cronkite with my Barbies each evening in front of the TV.

I was among the first generation of elementary school children in the United States to watch a nightly televised war. What seven-year-old grows accustomed to grenades exploding in horrific firefights and young men bleeding on stretchers? These were the disturbing images that taught me about the Vietnam conflict. *The Brady Bunch, I Love Lucy,* and *Mr. Ed,* the talking horse, were staples of my TV-watching years, and their happy-go-lucky images contrasted sharply with broadcasts of the war.

One day, in Mrs. Foster's fourth grade class, I approached a supply of magazines in a corner of the room used for art projects. Browsing through the glossy pages of an oversized *LIFE* magazine, I gasped when I saw the blood-soaked bodies of hundreds of innocent women and children—victims of the My Lai Massacre. Lieutenant William Calley, the American soldier who was later convicted of the atrocity, stared back at me in black and white. I felt like throwing up. I knew which side of the war I was on. My classmates and I purchased silver bracelets with the names of POWs. In a basement closet at home, I hung a door with strands of crepe paper, wore orange bell bottoms and love beads. I made poster boards to broadcast anti-war sentiments. U.S. OUT OF VIETNAM! I wrote in pink-and-black magic marker. GIVE PEACE A CHANCE!

After the fall of Saigon, TV coverage focused on heart-wrenching images of Vietnamese people hanging on to helicopters as aircraft lifted out of the nearly conquered city. News stories told of the "boat people" who fled Indochina on flimsy vessels to escape the oppressive Ho Chi Minh regime. Tens of thousands perished at sea or were attacked by Thai pirates. Those who sought to migrate to other countries came from Laos and Cambodia, as well as Vietnam.

Nhung Le's family had some money and waited for an opportunity to send Nhung Le and her sister to United States. The situation deteriorated to the point that they were willing to take a chance. There was a black market for food, clothing, and other items; living under the impoverished new order became unbearable. Finally, Nhung Le's father paid the equivalent of ten thousand dollars per person to get two of his daughters and four of his grandchildren (Nhung Le's sons) out of the country.

"When we got on the boat," Nhung Le explains, "I knew there was a 90 percent chance we die. The boat was not sturdy and we did not know where we were going. We had little food and water. We could not move at all. More than six hundred people were on board, too many for that boat."

On a sunny February afternoon thirty years after her escape from Vietnam, Nhung Le's sister, Le Grunewald (now a professor of Computer Science at the University of Oklahoma), sips tea in a Thai restaurant as she reflects on her life after the fall of Saigon and her subsequent immigration to the United States. Grunewald is a lovely woman who wears no jewelry except for a jade bangle given to her by her parents when she was a teenager. "One of the things I remember is the cultural inspectors visiting each house, removing 'objectionable' materials," she says, "particularly Western magazines, newspapers, or religious books. They ripped down my poster of Albert Einstein, my picture of Chopin, and a large photograph of Apollo 13 that NASA sent to me when I was eight.

"The police expected you to become a cultural inspector and do the same to others. In light of conditions like this, it does not frighten you too much to get on a boat that might sink off the coast of your homeland, a boat that might not make it to another shore. You must comprehend the desperation one feels in order to put one's life on the line, knowing you may never see your family again. Under these circumstances, living means so little to you, that you prefer to take the chance to die." She speaks these words and others without emotion.

When I comment on her amazing story of survival, she adds nonchalantly, "You would do the same."

While I doubt this, I say nothing. The questions I have about the logistics of the voyage seem impolite. *What was the cost of the ticket? What could passengers bring with them? What did people do to pass the time?* Before they left, Le's father painted the expensive jade bangle—the one she wears on her wrist to this day—with rust-colored nail polish to disguise its value. Like the other travelers, both sisters began the trip with clothing and provisions, but the boat began to fill with water the first day, and passengers threw possessions and food overboard to lighten the load. Men continuously bailed sea water with pots and pans. Elderly people grew sick and died, their bodies tossed into the ocean.

Nhung Le and her family traveled through rain, fog, time zones. How does one sit five days and nights on a boat that leaks, in rain and intense tropical heat, with four children, two boys pressed to each side as Nhung Le and her sister did? Finally I ask, "How did you go to the bathroom?" There is silence for a moment. Le looks at me solemnly, but compassionately, and in a soft voice says, "We did not have to go to the bathroom. We were starving." At one point Le became so sick that others carried her to the deck of the boat, and she lay there looking up at the clouds. "I was ready to die," she said. "I was happy."

But Le Grunewald lived. Eventually, the boat was towed to Malaysia, and Le, Nhung Le, and Nhung Le's children found themselves marooned behind the coiled barbed wire of a refugee camp. During this time, they were not allowed to walk outside the fence. Five months passed in a dangerously congested slum, where thousands of Vietnamese families remained for up to ten months, watching new boatloads of people arrive. Nhung Le and her boys lived in a tent amidst stifling heat. There was no school for the boys or anything to do while they waited for paperwork that would permit their exit. They were given meager rations and minimal medical care. Happily, though, they were able to send a letter in code, first to friends in France, who then sent it on to the family in Vietnam. "We are safe," the letter communicated in cryptic fashion. "We are in Malaysia."

As we continue our conversation at My Ngoc in Oklahoma City, Nhung Le fills in the rest of the story. After finally leaving Malaysia half a year later, the two sisters and the four boys received the welcome stamp on a document that allowed them to continue to Houston where another sister awaited their arrival. After the horror of the voyage and the excruciating months in the Malaysian camp, Nhung Le and her younger sister were a long way from living happily ever after; however, they discovered a few sweet curiosities in their new home. The most splendid novelty for Nhung Le was the Coke machine in the building where she took English lessons. It delighted her to put a quarter in the machine and hear the *tha thump* of the bottle exiting to the drop slot. Living in a Vietnamese section of the city and trying to learn English was particularly difficult because she was surrounded by people speaking her native language. Another new world fascination proved to be the freeways of Houston. Nhung Le loved the wide lanes of the concrete overpasses. Though she herself did not drive, she loved to ride at night at high speeds past the bright lights of the Texas metropolis.

While her parents were still in Vietnam and her husband remained imprisoned in Hanoi, Nhung Le decided to strike out on her own as a businesswoman. Hearing of a growing Asian district in Oklahoma City without a jewelry store, Nhung Le left Houston and the comfort of her sisters. "I was a third-generation jeweler and so I came north and opened My Ngoc, a store with the same name as my father's place in Quy Nhan. At first the American who owned the plaza did not want to rent to me. I showed him a picture of my brother's store in Houston." Nhung Le assured him, "It will look just like this one." After he saw Nhung Le was a good tenant, the American rented to other Vietnamese. To get her business going, Nhung Le went through the phone book, searching for Vietnamese, Laotian, and Chinese names. She sent a letter to each address, advertising her grand opening. And the people came to buy the jade and other jewelry they could not get unless they traveled to a larger city. Today My Ngoc is part of a small strip mall of Asian shops.

One night Nhung Le was robbed at gunpoint, her inventory taken from her just as the Communists had taken her father's stock in Quy Nhan. Four small boys were sleeping in the apartment behind My Ngoc. The thief tied her hands behind her back just as the North Vietnamese had tied the hands of so many South Vietnamese. Nhung Le feared her life was over, not because the thief would kill her but because without her inventory, she would have no way to make a living.

But as Nhung Le was in the habit of doing, she began again. Her parents helped to finance her restart and this single mother of four worked seven days a week to re-create her jewelry store. Years passed, and she grew comfortable in the Asian community in Oklahoma City where Indochinese groceries and restaurants began appearing and a Buddhist temple was built. The culture was a microcosm of the one she had left behind. Each day she rose at 5 A.M. to prepare Vietnamese food such as Ban Cuon (pork dumplings) and Hu Tien (a broth with noodles) for her children. Then she got them off to school and she went to work.

In 1983, Nhung Le's husband was released from prison in North Vietnam and he joined his family in the United States. Nhung Le jokes that she had to teach the children to say "daddy." When he arrived, the children didn't know how to relate to him.

They had not seen him in ten years. His wife hugged him, patted him, and pointed to him, this unusual specimen called a father. It took six months for them to grow accustomed to the soft-spoken man with the battle scars on his arms.

On Tuesdays in the summer, when the weather was pleasant, Nhung Le would close the store and the entire family would go to the zoo to watch animals in a full spectrum of colors: a swampy alligator tossing its prey to the sky and grabbing it in its long mouth on the way down; stunningly alert tuxedoed penguins and exotic green turtles sunning themselves. "It was then I felt at home," Nhung Le explains. "I felt security. I had my family and no Communist would knock on my door again."

These days it is Nhung Le who determines who enters her door and who does not. It has been ten years since I first rang the bell of My Ngoc and came into the house of beautiful jade. The Asian district is now a very different place than it was when Nhung Le arrived, when the only other business apart from hers was a small grocery across the way. Today Carson and I stop in at the Asian Wal-Mart of the strip, Super Cao Nguyen, where I buy him a chocolate-covered pretzel treat called Pocky. But who am I kidding? I hit every aisle in the shop. An hour later, I check out with pink lotus-flower teacups, sturdy straw mats for my kitchen, and a trendy bamboo plant for good luck.

Since I am nearby, I drop into Nhung Le's place to do further research. It is Saturday morning, and on weekends the café quality of My Ngoc is accentuated by the sharp tones of Vietnamese resonating throughout the store. I imagine people are talking about jobs and cars and what is on sale at the grocery store and how big the children have grown. Customers sit on stools in front of glass cases, entranced. In the corner is a black leather couch where men gather to drink tea while their wives point Nhung Le to a particular diamond or pearl.

Nhung Le moves gracefully around My Ngoc, her hair in a small pony tail, wearing a lavender jade figure around her neck and her signature wrist beads. This queen of merchants reigns over the party. Though the economy is bad, people come, as they always have, to buy her jewelry. I take a seat and spread my papers on the counter. Suddenly, she stands before me. "And what can I do for you ma'am?" She smiles. I take advantage of the moment she has offered, asking her to travel backward thirty years. But the Lady of Jade hasn't much time to reflect on the darkness of that era.

The buzzer rings. A young Vietnamese woman waves a gloved hand near the window, and Nhung Lee buzzes her into the jade refuge on the Boulevard. I wait for my friend to return as she always does, to talk with me about a life lived in Vietnam and Oklahoma along the margins of peace and war, poverty and prosperity. And in between the stories, I linger to watch Nhung Le show me a bangle or some inimitable pearl, as grand and extraordinary as her life.

Oklahoma rose rocks

The Ideal Home

⌒

In my early twenties, I entertained a brief but intense desire to live in New York City. I did not yet suffer from debilitating claustrophobia, so I could imagine myself on crowded streets where buildings rose to the sky in an urban conglomerate. A tiny Big Apple apartment with a view, like the one my bohemian friends rented in Manhattan, held debaucherous appeal. These boys and girls made a metropolitan lifestyle look easy: drinking all night, writing or acting by day, and bartending evenings before the party began. I was afflicted in late adolescence by a restlessness and self-destruction inspired by Sylvia Plath and Jack Kerouac, whose lives indicated that depression and drunkenness were useful for the sake of art. And where depression and drunkenness for the sake of art were concerned, New York seemed the place to be. Living in Columbus, Ohio, I was homesick for a home I had never known, one constructed mostly from a cinematic ideal. My dreams of living in New York were also strongly influenced by *Breakfast at Tiffany's*. Who could help but believe in a city where a naive, eccentric socialite named Holly Golightly makes her fortune by changing her name, walking everywhere in high-heeled shoes, transcending herself and all her previous connections?

When I landed, not in New York but in Oklahoma, I planned to blow on down the road like Panhandle tumbleweed, rolling toward a greater unknown. Some people spend their lives in search of changing weather and fresh landscapes. Like them, I intended to remain in motion. My arrival on the Oklahoma plains, however, collided with a certain middle-aged/New Aged understanding: *Wherever you go, there you are.* Adam Gopnik puts it more eloquently in *Paris to the Moon.* He says it is futile to try to outrun yourself by moving place to place: "the ghosts that haunted you in New York or Pittsburgh will haunt you anywhere you go, because they're your ghosts and the house they haunt is you."

Gradually I became aware the grass was no longer greener everywhere I wasn't. To my great relief, the envy quotient decreased in my new geography, a consequence of age or adaptation, I can't say for sure which. But in a region of abundant sunlight and precious little traffic, I grew increasingly, surprisingly content.

I took comfort from an exhaustive flatland and a horizon that was mostly sky. I could no longer ride in crowded elevators or buses or walk in the midst of large numbers of people without becoming dizzy and short of breath. I felt best in the openness around me. Even so, friends who came to visit Oklahoma were always taken back by the stark landscape. They said, "How can you live without trees?" While I always claimed to like trees as much as the next person, I came to realize I do prefer the prairie to the forest, to the mountains, to the ocean. But why? Was it simply a rebellious brain chemistry demanding more room?

Researchers in the interdisciplinary field of environmental psychology (or ecopsychology) have studied the reactions of people to their surroundings for decades. In the early 1970s, Harold Proshansky, one of the "fathers" of environmental psychology, explored the concept of *place identity* at City University of New York before neuroscience research became prominent. He and his colleagues argued that a profound relationship exists between our surroundings and our identity. Like our intimate social bonds, our relationship with the larger world is built from countless sensory interactions between ourselves and our settings. The places we live influence our plans of action, preferences, and emotional reactions in ways we probably don't suspect.

While the field now centers primarily on "built environments" and architects who design work spaces for enhanced productivity, geographers, sociologists, psychologists, and others continue to research the reactions human beings have to physical space—both natural and human-made. Most of the research is focused on the ways in which urban locations affect human beings. But some researchers continue to study place identity and the ways in which natural environments create a variety of responses in people who inhabit various terrains. Some scientists suggest that our relationship with nature is a hard-wired part of our brain, but how that relationship is expressed is, they claim, as varied as natural landscapes.

For some individuals, the home of childhood remains the cultural reference point; for others, home is encountered somewhere in future travels where the preferred topography creates a lucid map of comfort previously unknown. For each of us the idea of home is varied and profoundly symbolic; it is an idea that carries us through all of our comings and goings, a territorial core that anchors us no matter where we go. While the notion of home is for many people a domestic space, small as a favorite chair or a comforting room, for others it is a complex geographical mix of weather, people, and other habitual conditions that are tied to a particular locality.

Nicholas Howe writes that "in our migratory, dislocated time, home is rarely the same place as our native soil." The evolution of technology and communication has made it easier for some of us to uproot ourselves from our families and go where job advancement or impulse lead us. Some say that in our twenty-first-century Western societies, we have moved away from notions of home that are based on domesticity and the nuclear family to an individualistic concept of home that is based on lifestyle gratification. These days, commuter families are no longer an anomaly and technological innovations such as cell phones and Skyping promise us ever new ways to stay in touch. It is not unusual for spouses with very different notions of the ideal home to travel back and forth long distances to separate home bases, the marriage no worse for the wear and tear of the commute.

While the telephone made it possible for me to uproot myself from my childhood home and move 1500 miles west, since it allowed me to keep in contact with loved ones and friends, there were plenty of reasons why I thought I was just passing through. For one, Oklahoma has a tragic history: I didn't think I could live on the plains indefinitely because it would be like moving into a house with sad and desperate ghosts that rattled the shutters and distracted you from the view. Numerous horrors befell those who declared Indian Territory as their home. Heartbreak and hardship hang over the state like the red Dust Bowl clouds of the thirties. Indians were pushed here on the Trail of Tears; African Americans came to start a new life in numerous black towns where many met with racism and hardship. And while the covered wagon pulling into new territory is a legendary symbol in the empire-building narrative of the American West, how many pictures of sad white women standing beside dirt dugouts do you have to see before you realize that settling on the Great Plains was not exactly a piece of cake? Oklahoma's historical narrative is one of pain and exploitation—and all in the fairly recent past. The tragic search for home under such formidable circumstances suggests an unimaginably bleak and deeply disturbing portrait.

Take the example of homesteader and writer Caroline Henderson. After graduating from Mount Holyoke College in 1907, Henderson went to the Panhandle of Oklahoma in search of an independent life. She took a job at a school in Eva while she established a claim on a section of land near the local school. When a man named Will Henderson came to dig a well on her land, they began a courtship and married soon after. For the next fifty years, they tried to raise wheat and other crops in one of the most agriculturally challenging areas of the country. Facing drought, grasshopper plagues, and dust storms, Henderson began to supplement their meager farm livelihood through her writing. She wrote to the editor of *Ladies' World* magazine to ask how she might earn some money from her writing. Henderson's letter was filled with the trials of farming on the prairie, and the editor suggested that she continue to send dispatches from this desolate land under the signature "The Homestead Lady."

Between 1913 and 1918, Henderson wrote numerous accounts for *Ladies' World* of her life as a struggling farmer. During the 1930s, her work appeared more broadly—in *The Atlantic Monthly, Arizona Highways,* and other magazines. But the income her writing generated was not enough to save her family from the combined calamity of the Dust Bowl and the Depression. This is one of her accounts of nearly ten years' worth of dust storms she and her family experienced in the Oklahoma panhandle: "At the little country store of our neighborhood after one of the worst of these storms, the candies in the show case all look alike and equally brown . . . 'Dust to eat,' and dust to breathe and dust to drink. Dust in the beds and in the flour bin, on dishes and walls and windows, in hair and eyes and ears and teeth and throats, to say nothing of the heaped up accumulation on floors and window sills."

Although Henderson and her husband remained on their land until 1965, the challenges she and her family faced made her feel like a failure and ultimately compromised her faith and personal optimism. But her refusal to leave her home, like countless others who remained in Oklahoma during the Dust Bowl, demonstrates that migration is not the only, or even most important, Oklahoma story.

The refusal of so many Oklahomans to leave the state is the story that most people did not consider after *The Grapes of Wrath* made the theme of migration the major Oklahoma story of the twentieth century. The people who sustained a life on the Great Plains are of greatest interest to me; they make me proud of the state and its history. It is clear that Oklahoma has many cultures and many kinds of people who have built something distinct and wonderful. The people of this region have been instrumental in generating an Oklahoma plains country culture in art, cooking, music, architecture, and other elements shaped by geography and adaptation.

When I realized that I could not remake an Ohio garden in Oklahoma, I learned to adapt—and began a long series of adaptations that would render me Okie. My attempts to grow bleeding hearts and stately foxglove were thwarted by gusts that toppled my plants like fallen soldiers. After too many casualties of this sort, I hauled fewer truckloads of compost to mix with the crusty orange clay, working less fervently to improve the soil that challenges every gardener in this region. Too often much of the compost blew off the top anyway before I could work it into the squash-colored earth. I let my garden go its own way, a little wilder and more rugged than my eastern terrain. It was easy to give up on a certain ideal after a realization I had when driving along a stretch of country where no one would ever *think* of planting an English garden. What I witnessed helped me appreciate this stark and spare aesthetic—the role played by rock, wind, and sky. I observed a solitary ranch house (with a characteristically Oklahoma windmill on the acreage). There were two or three pieces of weathered-metal yard furniture and rocks scattered around. The blue sky, pulling lilac clouds overhead, was the most significant aspect of this prairie garden. Everything about the view said: *lose ornament; lose clutter, lose order.* And so I did.

Instead of delphinium and aster, I added plants native to the region like Indian blanket and yarrow and dared the wind to press them to the ground. I placed statuesque red rocks where delicate flowers had dropped. These craggy ornaments stood against the gusts in rusted glory. I pressed rose rocks, large and small, into the soil in mosaic fashion; their stone petals remain in bloom no matter the weather. A geological curiosity, the rose rock forms in only two counties in all of Oklahoma. Although a lighter, coral-colored version of the rock can be found in Texas, California, and Egypt, there is no explanation for why the crimson rocks are common in this region.

One legend explains Oklahoma's rose rock phenomenon in tragic terms. It claims that on the Trail of Tears trek to Oklahoma, God turned the blood of Indian braves and the tears of the maidens to stone. The legend is printed on the packaging of rose rock earrings, necklaces, and refrigerator magnets, but American Indians say the legend is not theirs—just another exploitation of Indians in order to sell regional wares. Wherever rose rocks come from, they have become a signature of Oklahoma gardens and porches everywhere. They offer a delicate but sturdy look. In August, when the heat renders my rose bushes mute, rose rocks offer up their sandstone petals—in glistening crimson—to remind me that stone blossoms can be dug from the ground, a floral treasure.

Just as I have begun to appreciate a new mode of gardening, I have come to admire the music that has emerged from of this region. If, as Kathleen Norris says, the prairie is still waiting for its own Georgia O'Keeffe to paint the essence of the plains, it already has those who champion it in song. I have discovered just how happy I can be driving around the prairie in a pickup, listening to the music made famous by Oklahomans. More famous country music artists hail from Oklahoma than almost any other state, including many powerhouses in contemporary country music: Reba McEntire, Joe Diffey, Vince Gill, J.J. Cale, and, of course, Garth Brooks, whose fame Yukon, Oklahoma, blasts from its water tower just off I-40. I read recently that if a country station deejay chose not to play a single song by any artist born in Oklahoma, or any who spent an appreciable period within the borders of the state, 60 percent of the programming would be summarily removed from the playlist.

Famous musicians who have their roots in Oklahoma include Gene Autry, Wanda Jackson, Patti Page, Roger Miller, Leon Russell, and the legendary Woody Guthrie, whose "This Land Is Your Land" is something of a national anthem. It gave me such a thrill when I first moved here to drive around the prairie, whirling the dial past so much church radio to bring in the music that pays tribute to the region. When you listen to Don Williams's "Livin' on Tulsa Time," David Frizzell and Shelly West's "You're the Reason God Made Oklahoma," or Merle Haggard's "Okie from Muskogee," you can't help but feel that Oklahoma really is someplace to sing about.

Not every resident, though, shares the reverence for these and other musicians of this territory—nor can they easily make a home here. My husband, whose roots are strictly midwestern, moved to the region sight unseen. When I encouraged him to visit the state before I accepted a job at the University of Oklahoma, he shrugged his shoulders and replied with adventurous bravado, "Hey—it's America. How different from Ohio can it really be?" He later regretted that statement and the decision not to preview his new locale, finding his adopted home to be such a foreign place that he often wondered how it ever became part of the United States at all. Frank complains of poorly constructed roads, corrupt politics, and an economy lagging behind nearly every other state in the union. Once, when trying to account for his difficulty adjusting to the prairie, he placed his hands squarely on my shoulders as he explained in a somber ME TARZAN, YOU JANE fashion: "We are Great Lakes people." He spoke these words with dramatic effect, as though it were a known fact that no one from Indiana, Illinois, Michigan, or Ohio could ever be happy on the plains. My husband is not alone in this conviction. The child of a colleague shares Frank's sentiments, including the view that Oklahoma may not really be part of the United States after all. Observing the differences between Oklahoma and the East Coast, where he had spent most of his young life, six-year-old Nathan one day announced to his mother shortly after moving to Norman, "Mommy, I don't like it here. Can we go back to America?"

Over the years, I've been drawn to people who greet the landscape that some see as barren and desolate with enthusiasm and affection. One of my more erudite colleagues came to Norman in 1967, before the town boasted much in the way of commerce or urban comforts. Alan Velie is a Jewish New Yorker, educated at Harvard and Stanford—a man who, even after forty years on the Great Plains, appears quite eastern in the tweed blazers he sports in professorial fashion. His father was a writer for *The Saturday Evening Post,* a man who lunched with presidents and East Coast intellectuals. Yet when Alan moved to Oklahoma in the late sixties, he loved it immediately.

"I grew up in Queens," he told me one day, "listening to the *Lone Ranger* on the radio. When the radio announcer said *this program is brought to you by Kelloggs in Battle Creek, Michigan,* I thought of Michigan as a western place. Enchanted by those words and that radio show, the West loomed large in my imagination. When I first came to Oklahoma, I bought a horse, but I couldn't afford a saddle; and so I learned to ride bareback."

The image of my New Yorker colleague on a horse with no saddle is amusing, but it's also an indicator of how some people thrive where others fade in a new environment. My guess is that when Professor Velie retires, he will not simply pack up and move back east as so many of my retired colleagues have done. His roots and his family are now in Oklahoma, and he will not leave a community of friends he has known for over forty years.

Others had to leave Oklahoma before they could claim it as home. The writer Rilla Askew, famous for her Oklahoma stories, left the state when she was young to pursue an acting career in New York City. It wasn't until she had been gone some time and had chosen a writer's path instead that she realized the most interesting stories she had to tell were about a place she had been determined to leave forever.

Like Askew, many of my students are eager to make their way out of the state and into what they believe to be more vibrant parts of the country. Who could blame them? Some are embarrassed to have been born here at all; others simply wish to explore the larger world and return someday. However, the lack of pride some native Oklahomans feel about the state makes me sad, only because I know how much cultural inferiority can contribute to a low regard of one's self. In a course I teach called *Reading and Writing Oklahoma: Region and Representation,* I always ask students at the beginning of the semester how many of them are native Oklahomans. Out of sixteen or seventeen students, there are always a few who claim to have been born elsewhere. By the end of the course, these outliers will acknowledge that they were born in Texas, or some other nearby state, but they moved to Oklahoma when they were a few months old and have lived here ever since. Yes, they confess; they are native Oklahomans too.

Students are shocked when I tell them that I envy their native status, because, to some extent, I will always be an outsider here. Only I think it matters less where a person is born than where he or she *can* live. I imagine cities where I would experience an emotionally impoverished existence, where smog, traffic, and an overall industrial climate would depress me on a daily basis. And so, turning the situation around, I understand that not everyone can live where there are so few trees, in a place where grass fires and tornadoes threaten every spring.

Perhaps without the women I've met here who have taught me to see that Oklahoma is far more than "flyover country," I might have moved before I saw that I was invited to feast on lilac sunsets, Route 66 architecture, and illuminated prairie grass circling country ponds in halo fashion.

But Oklahoma is more than what you see. If you listen, you will hear language put on a fine show. People tell me I now pronounce one syllable words like *pill* as *pe-ill* and *school* as *sku-ool.* At one time I might have looked down these pronunciations.

But there is nothing stupid about people who can generate an infinite number of linguistically delightful phrases. "He's not her first rodeo," a woman says in a store one day, speaking of the string of men who have broken her daughter's heart. A cashier at the IGA complains to another cashier about her fatigue and confusion: "I don't know if it's Tuesday or Main Street." I eavesdrop with relish on other conversations, celebrating all the ways that language can turn.

"We've talked it all the way to Kansas and back," my friend Rachel says to me one evening after a long, spirited phone conversation. And so we had. I have collected these lines over the years and put them to good use. Like patchwork quilts made by Oklahoma women, I now possess a splendid and sundry mosaic of language, lovely as pieced scraps of cloth.

Each year, *USA Today*, *Money Magazine*, and a host of other publications rank what they believe are the ideal locations to reside. They base their findings on a variety of criteria, not the least of which are healthcare, air quality, job availability, and real estate prices. Most of Oklahoma is pretty far down the list, if it is on the list at all. Over the years I have watched my share of new colleagues come to this university town from east and west and find they could not adjust to this peculiar region after years of urban living. Perhaps it was the distance from the ocean or the stifling high summer temperatures, or the quirky intensity of the Bible Belt. In the end, I couldn't blame them for their inability to make a life here, and so I have waved good-bye to more than a few friends who were happy to shake the dust of Oklahoma from their shoes.

I have, however, put roots down in this section of the Great Plains, flawed as it is. The logic of geography is as illogical as love. While it is pleasant to dream of an ideal home, a place with consistently temperate weather, stunning ocean views, and model citizens who never irritate you, I have come to realize that my ideal home is imperfect, charming in its imperfections, cherishable in the ways, if we are lucky, our friends and family cherish us in spite of ourselves.

Some see nothing remarkable about this section of the Oklahoma plains. To them, the open lands are a truly plain country—void of the exotic beauty on which travel writers dote. Ironically, I have longed for Oklahoma from some of the places most celebrated by travel writers. From Paris, Rome, or Amsterdam, I have missed the red dirt in the sunlight or a wide expanse of sky that has no equal.

The prairie stretches north and south and east and west of me like a sea. Here, in the middle of the United States, I feel anchored and adrift, lost and found, at the center of everything and nothing. The wind presents itself to me as a messenger, carrying something intangible from another territory. I have harnessed the wind's artistic power, adding clusters of tall grass in my garden that arch and sway like hula dancers. The wind lends a visual dimension to the yard as well as an aural one. Three sets of chimes on my back porch *chingle* and *ling* throughout the day, sometimes violently. When temperatures move past one hundred degrees, the chimes are soothing, like ice cubes in a glass. These wind-induced tones are now part of my garden, and the vigorous motion of these instruments also warns of approaching storms, adding a particular drama to thunder when it comes.

On a summer night, pumping gas at 11 P.M. when the gusts are still warm, I stare at the darkness on the other side of the bright lights streaming down on the Texaco parking lot. A hot wind blows in from the west and I wonder if it has rustled the hair of a baby in New Mexico or pushed more cellophane wrappers and lipstick-stained coffee cups my direction. This much I always know for sure: even in the dark we are in the open. On the Great Plains there are few towns and hardly any cities that dot the vast grassland to act as a brake on whatever chooses to blow through. It is a good home for waiting on weather, wind, or whatever might come next. We know that whether we watch for June bugs, storm clouds, or red dirt whirling—in Oklahoma, the wind is a messenger, a sign that something is always on its way.

References

⁓

EPIGRAPH

Cisneros, Sandra. *The House on Mango Street*. New York: Vintage, 1991.

INTRODUCTION: PRAIRIE WOMEN, PRAIRIE PLACES

Dinesen, Isak. *Out of Africa*. New York: Modern Library, 1992.

Fisher, Ada Lois Sipuel, and Danney Goble. *A Matter of Black and White: The Autobiography of Ada Lois Sipuel Fisher*. Foreword by Robert Henry. Norman: University of Oklahoma Press, 1996.

Henderson, Caroline. *Letters from the Dust Bowl*. Edited by Alvin O. Turner. Norman: University of Oklahoma Press, 2001.

Leckie, Shirley A. *Angie Debo: Pioneering Historian*. Norman: University of Oklahoma Press, 2000.

Mankiller, Wilma, and Michael Wallis. *Mankiller: A Chief and Her People*. New York: St. Martin's Griffin, 1999.

Musslewhite, Lynn, and Suzanne Jones Crawford. *One Woman's Political Journey: Kate Barnard and Social Reform, 1875–1930*. Norman: University of Oklahoma Press, 2003.

Reese, Linda Williams. *Women of Oklahoma, 1890–1920*. Norman: University of Oklahoma Press, 1997.

Schackel, Sandra K., ed. *Western Women's Lives: Continuity and Change in the Twentieth Century*. Albuquerque: University of New Mexico Press, 2003.

ADOPTION STORY

Cole, Joanna. *How I Was Adopted: Samantha's Story.* Illustrated by Maxie Chambliss. New York: Harper Trophy, 1999.

Curtis, Jamie Lee. *Tell Me again about the Night I Was Born.* Illustrated by Laura Cornell. New York: Harper Collins, 2000.

Girard, Linda Walvoord. *Adoption is for Always.* Illustrated by Judity Friedman. Chicago: Whitman, 1991.

GREAT PLAINS SALVAGE

Frank, Donna. *Clay in the Master's Hands.* New York: Vantage Press, 1977.

Margolies, John. *The End of the Road: Vanishing Highway Architecture in America.* New York: Penguin, 1981.

Scott, Quinta. *Along Route 66.* Norman: University of Oklahoma Press, 2001.

MISS DORRIE AT BIG SKY

Gross, Jane. "No Talking out of Preschool; Favoritism in Nursery School Entrance? No Comment." *New York Times.* November 15, 2002.

Robicheaux, Beau C. "The Kindergarten Ivy League." *Harvard Crimson.* April 14, 2005.

GIRLS IN THE RING

Kasper, Shirl. *Annie Oakley.* Norman: University of Oklahoma Press, 1992.

Riley, Glenda. *The Life and Legacy of Annie Oakley.* Norman: University of Oklahoma Press, 1994.

Rule, Dona Kay. Personal interview. January 10, 2008.

Savage, Candace. *Cowgirls.* Vancouver: Greystone Books, 1996.

Teehee, Tiffany. Personal interview. January 17, 2008.

Williams, Sallye. Personal interview. January 17, 2008.

Wilson, Ellen, and Jerry Robinson. *Annie Oakley: Little Sure Shot.* Illustrated by Vance Locke. Indianapolis: Bobbs-Merrill, 1962.

Wallis, Michael. *The Real Wild West: The 101 Ranch and the Creation of the American West.* New York: St. Martin's Griffin, 2000.

THE BIRD WATCHER

Jackson, Jerome A. *George Miksch Sutton: Artist, Scientist, and Teacher.* Norman: University of Oklahoma Press, 2007.

Sutton, George Miksch. *Fifty Common Birds of Oklahoma and the Southern Great Plains.* Norman: University of Oklahoma Press, 1981.

The Birds. Directed by Alfred Hitchcock. Universal Studios, 1963.

CASINOLAND

Cobb, Jacy. Personal interview. May 9, 2008.

QUEENS OF THE PIONEER OUTBACK

Bridges, Bill. Videotape, 1995.

Egan, Timothy. *The Worst Hard Time: The Untold Story of Those Who Survived the Great American Dustbowl.* New York: Mariner Books, 2006.

Frazier, Ian. *Great Plains.* New York: Penguin, 1989.

Henderson, Arn, Frank Parman, and Dortha Henderson. *Architecture in Oklahoma: Landmark and Vernacular.* Norman: Point Riders, 1978.

ROLLER DOLLS

Blood on the Flat Track: The Rise of the Rat City Rollergirls. Directed by Lainy Bagwell and Lacey Leavitt. Leaky-Sleazewell Productions, 2007.

Joulwan, Melissa "Melicious." *Rollergirl: Totally True Tales from the Track.* New York: Simon & Schuster, 2007.

Tornado Alley Rollergirls. Personal Interviews. November 11, 2010.

Whip It. Directed by Drew Barrymore. 20th Century Fox, 2009.

LADY OF JADE

Grunewald, Le. Personal Interview. February 8, 2010.

Nguyen, Nhung Le. Personal Interview. January 9, 2010.

THE IDEAL HOME

Frazier, Ian. *Great Plains.* New York: Penguin, 1989.

Gallagher, Winifred. *The Power of Place: How Our Surroundings Shape Our Thoughts, Emotions and Actions.* New York: Harper Collins, 1994.

Gopnik, Adam. *Paris to the Moon.* New York: Random House, 2001.

Heimstra, Norman W., and Leslie H. McFarling. *Environmental Psychology.* Monterey, Calif.: Brooks/Cole, 1974.

Howe, Nicholas. *Across an Inland Sea: Writing in Place from Buffalo to Berlin.* Princeton: Princeton University Press, 2003.

Johnson, Hannibal B. *Acres of Aspiration: The All-Black Towns in Oklahoma.* Austin: Eakin Press, 2003.

Klein, Joe. *Woody Guthrie: A Life.* New York: Knopf, 1980.

Norris, Kathleen. *Dakota: A Spiritual Geography.* New York: Houghton Mifflin, 2001.

Proshansky, Harold. Environmental Psychology: Man and His Physical Setting. New York: Holt, Rinehart and Winston, 1970.

Wallis, Michael. *Way Down Yonder in the Indian Nation: Writings from America's Heartland.* New York: St. Martin's Griffin, 1993.

Acknowledgments

I am grateful to Frank Kates, Carson Kates, and the rest of my family for their support and encouragement throughout the writing of this book.

Thanks to members of my writing group, Matt Bokovoy, Catherine Hobbs, Paula Sullivan, and the late Kirk Bjornsgaard, who saw this project through the early stages. Rick Brown, Jay Dew, Rachel Jackson, David Levy, Barbara Lounsberry, Ron Schleifer, and Jackie Spangler provided keen insights and helped me rethink and revise my work along the way.

Special thanks to Rilla Askew for reading and commenting on the manuscript for this book, for writing the foreword, and for her Oklahoma stories, which have enriched my own.

I am indebted to Debbie Colson at The No Man's Land Museum for her guidance on the history of the Oklahoma Panhandle; to Kathleen Kelly, editor at the University of Oklahoma Press, for her help with all facets of this book; and to my students in *Reading and Writing Oklahoma: Region and Representation*, for new ideas they offered to me regarding Oklahoma culture.

I am grateful to Alice Stanton, special projects editor at OU Press, whose brilliant and meticulous editing has made this book a more graceful tribute to Oklahoma women.

Thanks to the editors of the journals and publications in which the following essays, in different versions, first appeared: "Adoption Story," in *PoemMemoirStory* (2007); "Girls in the Ring," in *Big Muddy* (2008); and "The Bird Watcher," in *Ain't Nobody That Can Sing Like Me* (2010).

Finally, I wish to thank the Oklahoma women who shared their experiences with me so that I could see Oklahoma in new ways. These women have given me far more than a book. They have helped me find my home.